WALKING THROUGH THE WEEDS

Exploring the Source of
Blessings and Curses

Lawrence S. Perry

WESTBOW
P R E S S
A DIVISION OF THOMAS NELSON

WestBow Press books may be ordered through booksellers or by contacting:

WestBow Press
A Division of Thomas Nelson
1663 Liberty Drive
Bloomington, IN 47403
www.westbowpress.com
1-(866) 928-1240

Because of the dynamic nature of the Internet, any web addresses or links contained in this book may have changed since publication and may no longer be valid. The views expressed in this work are solely those of the author and do not necessarily reflect the views of the publisher, and the publisher hereby disclaims any responsibility for them.

Any people depicted in stock imagery provided by Thinkstock are models, and such images are being used for illustrative purposes only.

Certain stock imagery © Thinkstock.

ISBN: 978-1-4497-5931-5 (sc)
ISBN: 978-1-4497-5932-2 (hc)
ISBN: 978-1-4497-5930-8 (e)

Library of Congress Control Number: 2012912229

Printed in the United States of America

WestBow Press rev. date: 08/13/2012

Contents

To my incredible wife, Margretta, and my children, Andrina and Tony, who have inspired my insights.

INTRODUCTION

O NE of the great mysteries of the New Testament is that it is veiled in the confusion of paradox. As we read the Scriptures, we can easily become perplexed because that which appears to be false turns out to be true and that which is true reveals itself as false.

We don't have to go far into the Bible to encounter this strange truth. For example, when Jesus hung on the cross on that fateful afternoon we call Good Friday, he was thought to be cursed by the very words that originated from his Father. In the Old Testament, all who were hung on a tree were cursed (Deut. 21:23). Consequently, Orthodox Jews of Jesus' day could not possibly consider him the Messiah because the cross could not be an instrument of blessing. God, through his Word, had already declared the verdict. Yet it is through this "curse" that humankind was redeemed and restored in the kingdom and was able to reestablish a relationship with God the Father.

This strange mystery is not only found in the story of the passion. These inexplicable stories continue from the book of Genesis and beyond. In the New Testament, we again encounter the great paradox in the many teachable moments of Jesus. One parable that speaks to this truth is the parable of the wheat and the weeds (Matt. 13).

In this revealing story, Jesus is attempting to inform his disciples of the nature of the kingdom of God. He is not only presenting a theological insight; he's teaching a lesson about life. So in a tranquil setting next to the Sea of Galilee, Jesus exposes the paradox with a simple story. Perhaps in the distance, he saw a farmer's field of wheat. Pointing to the wheat field, he says, "Look. The kingdom of God is like that wheat field over there." Having piqued their interest, he elaborates and captures the attention of his audience as they move closer to hear his every word.

Jesus tells the story: A farmer sowed some good seed in that field, but while he was sleeping one night, his enemy slithered through the darkness and spread darnel in the midst of the wheat. Jesus' audience immediately knew the consequences. Darnel was commonly known as a nocuous weed in the time of Jesus. In fact, this weed was deadly if consumed by humans. Furthermore, darnel was extremely problematic because when it first sprouted, no one could distinguish it from the wheat, as the weed and the wheat looked alike. To complicate matters, when the wheat and weeds grew side by side, their roots would intertwine. So if you attempted to pull out the weed, you risked pulling out the wheat as well. The paradox was now clear: That which was good, wholesome, and brought life could not be distinguished from that which was deadly.

This lesson, in all probability, captivated Jesus' audience. They were all most likely thinking about how one can distinguish and choose between that which can bring life and that which can bring death. Everyone could see the puzzling dilemma.

That which seems puzzling to the human observer, however, is quite clear in the mind of the Christ. The solution was simple: patience! Why? Jesus tells those who had gathered that one must allow the wheat and weeds to grow together, and when they have matured, the weed can be identified for what it is. Then, at the harvest, the wheat and weeds can be separated. The weeds will be gathered, and because they offer no benefit to the community, they will be destroyed. But the wheat will be allowed to fulfill its purpose, feeding and nurturing those who gather its golden treasure.

This powerful lesson lays the foundation for understanding the nature of blessings and curses in those moments in our lives that prove to be most challenging. As a result, we are hurt physically, emotionally, and spiritually by people and situations we encounter on a daily basis. In this wake of destruction, we are left damaged, depressed, and confused because we cannot see clearly to distinguish that which will be a blessing and that which will be a curse. We stand with blurred vision, not knowing as we live out life's drama which is the wheat and which are the weeds.

This book is an invitation to take a short walk with me into a field that is filled with weeds and wheat. As we walk, we will look for answers along the way. Many times, we will find ourselves standing at the edge of the field, wondering which path leads to blessing and which leads to curse. In such moments, the Scriptures will be our map, and we will discover the signs along the way that will lead us to the truth. In this living drama, we will discover the steps that move us from the weeds into the wheat. When we are unsure of ourselves and are too timid to take the next step, we will learn how to use and call upon guides to lead us on our journey. Equally important, we will discover that the choices we make and the steps we take move us into God's perfect will and his blessings. In this wonderful and mysterious journey filled with paradox, we will uncover God's grace and his presence.

Chapter One

THE WORLD OF PARADOX

IN looking into the world of blessings and curses, one of the topics to explore is the world of paradox. Without understanding this world, you will be left confused and frustrated. The confusion begins when you take some action in your life that you think will lead to a blessing, only to find yourself cursed by your efforts. Then, as you continue in this strange world of paradox, you enter a situation thinking you have been cursed—only to discover that the curse has evolved into a blessing. This great paradox is played out every day of our lives; no one can escape this reality. A humorous example of this paradox was televised in an episode of *Seinfeld*, a sitcom that revolved around Jerry Seinfeld, a New York City comedian, who plays himself.

Jerry interacts with three of his best friends: George, Elaine, and Kramer. Each person has his or her own unique character and a role that adds brilliance to the program. The show does not have an ongoing plot; rather, it chronicles the daily lives of these four New Yorkers. The program was very successful and ran for a number of years on television, garnering many TV awards. One of the reasons for its success was that every now and then an episode would strike gold. It bordered on genius, revealing the nature of the human heart. One episode was a story about opposites.

In the episode, George enters Monk's Restaurant, and as usual, he is his grumpy old self. From the moment he sits down, he complains to Jerry and Elaine that his life is going nowhere. Everything that George does seems to be wrong. Every life decision takes him down the road to disaster. Although not spoken out loud, you look at George and think, *This is a man who is cursed!* Moreover, George just does not get it. He has not figured out why he keeps making the same poor choices in life.

As George rambles on, offering his tale of woe, Jerry listens patiently and, in a moment of profound wisdom, blurts out a solution. He tells George that if every inclination he has is wrong, the solution is simple. All George needs to do is the opposite! George considers this for a moment, and suddenly, the lights turn on. Jerry is right. Just then, Elaine notices a young, beautiful blonde staring at George. So Elaine nudges George, advises him of her observation, and encourages him to go talk to her. At first, he is hesitant. You know what he is thinking. Why would such a beautiful woman be interested in a short, stocky bald man who is out of a job and lives with his parents? Jerry and Elaine, however, encourage him to test his newfound revelation.

George gets out of the booth and walks over to the counter where the young woman is sitting. After a brief exchange of words, George takes the big step. He tells this young beauty that his name is George, he's unemployed, and he lives with his parents. For the first time, he is totally honest—unlike the old George. The young woman accepts the introduction with a big smile and says, "Hi! My name is Victoria."

Amazingly, George wins the affection of the girl, and for the rest of the program, he does everything against his old nature. In doing so, he begins a new life, telling people exactly what he thinks and feels. But rather than getting him into trouble or being rebuffed, he receives one blessing after another. With this newfound persona, George even gets his dream job with the New York Yankees with Victoria's help. Consequently, George begins living a blessed life— that is, until he resumes his old character in the next episode. Once again, George must endure the curses that he brings upon himself.

This brilliant episode of *Seinfeld* captures a unique truth that eludes many in our culture today. We live in a world that is veiled in a mysterious paradox. In the world of blessing and curses, there is a thin line that separates the two—and they often cross over. You know the story: you attempt to live a righteous life, thinking that such actions will open a cornucopia of good fortune and God's favor. Then, when those blessings mysteriously turn into curses, we are left, confused and hurt. *I did all the right things; why did my actions turn into such a disaster?* Then when that puzzling disaster has left us in ruins, we learn that if we are patient and wise, somehow the disaster can grow into a blessing. The experience is like standing in a field without knowing whether we are in the midst of the wheat or the weeds.

When we stop to think about it, this intriguing world of opposites is discovered in many of life's situations. Take, for example, the sacred stories in the

Scriptures. One such example is the calling of David to be king of Israel. The story unfolds after the Lord was greatly displeased with the actions of King Saul. In 1 Samuel 16, we find the details of this surprising story. Samuel, the prophet, was commissioned by the Lord to find a replacement for King Saul.

Samuel was ordered to go to Bethlehem to seek out the household of Jesse. There, Samuel would be further directed and instructed. When Samuel finds Jesse and invites him and his family to a sacrifice, we again encounter this strange world of paradox. As the sons of Jesse walk past the prophet, he first meets Eliab. This young man makes a strong impression on Samuel; he thinks that the Lord surely has chosen this one because he was tall in stature and strong. *How could he not be the one?* God says, "Do not look at his outer appearance or his height of stature, because I have rejected him" (v.7).

All seven sons pass before Samuel, but the Lord rejects each of them. Frustrated, Samuel asks Jesse, "Are these all of your sons?" Samuel reveals that the youngest is out tending the sheep. This is a clue to the reader that this youngest child is at the bottom of the pecking order. Why else would he be excluded from participating in this event? Someone had to attend to the sheep; would it not be the son who is least likely to be chosen? When David arrives, however, Samuel hears the voice of God clearly. "The youngest of the brothers is the one who shall be anointed." The mystery of why the least likely is chosen is quickly revealed.

God tells Samuel that people are prone to look at outward appearances. He looks deep into their hearts. That which he sees, thinks, and feels may well be the opposite of what we may think and feel. We will see this point made again as God reminds us that our ways are not his ways—and our thoughts are not his thoughts. His thinking and reasoning goes far beyond what we can conceive or envision, which leaves the door open to a world of contrasts (Isa. 55:8).

In the New Testament, we encounter one of the most powerful examples of living in the world of paradox in an explosive moment of the gospel. This example is so revolutionary that every generation from the time of Christ until now has had to wrestle with the implications and struggles to incorporate this teaching into their lives.

In the Hebrew culture, the world of opposites was well defined and clearly marked. Hebrew law clearly separated good from evil, black from white, and blessings from curses. As long as the righteous obeyed the law, they were assured of living in God's glory and reaping the benefits of his blessings.

According to Jewish thought, if a person was blessed with wealth, health, position, and children, they were thought to be blessed. No one would question that they were looked upon with favor from the most high. The poor, sick, widows, and orphans were a different matter. Since many of them had to scrape by to survive, they often lived lives that were looked upon as unclean. These people lived as outcasts. Their social status resulted in the fact that they could not always live up to the strict demands of the law as they eked out a living. Their salvation, therefore, was left in question. Why? It was well established in Hebrew theology at that point in history that the law was the means to reach righteousness. If you have any doubt, just read Psalm 119.

As we turn to the New Testament, we enter the contrarian world of Jesus. The Sermon on the Mount turns the Hebrew world upside down. Matthew records these revolutionary words in the fifth chapter of his gospel in the Sermon on the Mount. Many theologians have argued about whether or not this teaching could be practically lived out in one's life.

Some scholars believe that the Sermon on the Mount was an ideal for which we strive; others teach that these precepts are attainable. Many theologians agree that the sermon was consolidated from many teachings and edited into one. Nevertheless, this teaching remains one of the most powerful of Jesus' lessons.

In this teaching, he outlines the seven principles of blessing that lead us into the kingdom. The first lesson, perhaps shocking at the time, was that the rich did not inherit the kingdom per se, but it was open to those who were poor in spirit. In this teaching, Jesus is making a contrast between those who have everything and those who have nothing. Jesus, however, was not condemning wealth; he was drawing attention to attitudes. What the poor in spirit have that the rich may lack is a need to reach out to a power greater than themselves. Those who are poor in spirit hunger for God's word. They seek to be seated at a banquet table of wisdom, and they open their ears so they can consume the words that offer eternal life—unlike the rich who see themselves as self-sufficient. The poor recognize the need for a savior!

The second principle of blessing, which leads one into the kingdom, addresses those who mourn. Grief is one of the paradoxical emotions that affect both body and soul. None of us readily embraces grief. Grief hurts! We, therefore, try to deny its claim on our lives. We try to suppress it as best we can and push it to the deepest recesses of our hearts where it won't show. When we encounter someone in deep grief, we often feel badly because we are at a loss for words because we cannot fix the problem. This helplessness leads to a loss of hope. Yet, God has given the gift of tears to those who mourn as a gentle reminder that we must let go of the hurt that possesses us. Yes, we grieve, but our weeping has value.

These tears are the beginning of a process that is healthy and necessary for cleansing the human spirit. Think for a moment about getting a small particle in your eye. Your body immediately reacts with tears to help expel that foreign object. Could it be that this physiological reaction informs us that weeping is a necessary part of living? More importantly, we can extrapolate that which takes place physically also needs to take place emotionally. Weeping takes us to the place where we begin to deal with our loss rather than holding on to those raw emotions that can fester in our hearts and spirits with no way to heal.

Over the many years I spent in active ministry, I sat through my share of lectures on the grief process. In each lecture, the lecturer would address unresolved grief and its consequences. These unhealthy consequences often disguise themselves as anger, anxiety, depression, or self-destructive behavior. There are also some clinicians who will go further and argue that unresolved grief will lead to physical problems such as hypertension, heart disease, or other painful bodily aliments. The situation that causes us the most problems and raises the most havoc in our lives is the death of a loved one.

We can mourn many things, but death of a loved one is one of the most difficult to heal. Yet death gives us good reason to mourn. It was a tradition in ancient Jewish culture when death claimed a loved one to enter a long mourning process. These actions included beating your breast and tearing your clothing.

Consequently, when Jesus said, "Blessed are those who mourn," his audience must have thought he was crazy! What Jesus knew that his audience did not comprehend at the time, was that the divine mercy of God was about to cast its protective wings over all humanity. Mourning would therefore become an emotion that would no longer lay claim to our lives.

Through the death and resurrection of the Christ, death would release its grip over humankind.

In Revelation 7:17, we hear that the Lamb of God shall wipe every tear from every eye. Furthermore, St. Paul takes this thought, weaves it into his theology, and turns this idea into a veil of hope with great conviction.

The jars of clay contain the power of renewal.

> We are hard pressed on every side, but not
> crushed; perplexed, but not despairing;
> persecuted, but not abandoned, struck
> down but not destroyed; we always carry
> around in our body the death of Jesus, so
> that the life of Jesus may also be revealed
> in our mortal body. (2 Cor. 4:8f)

The third principle of the kingdom requires the adoption of a gentle spirit. In some translations, the word gentle is replaced by "humble" or "meek." With this precept, we are once again thrown into the world of paradox. In our culture, those who are humble or meek are often looked upon as if they have a character flaw. We don't embrace meekness; we would rather attach ourselves to the virile and strong. We lift up and honor the men and women who rise up through their acts of power. What did Jesus see in gentleness, humility, or meekness?

The key to understanding this paradox is to closely examine the life of Jesus. His humility was not his weakness; it was the means by which he grew in power and wisdom. We are reminded over and over again in the gospel that Jesus was always submissive to God his Father. Out of pure devotion, Jesus allowed the Spirit of God to work through him. This triad of being—the Trinity—will have unity of purpose, harmony, and equality. The result is a synergy that grows in power. Consequently, there are no obstacles to block the will of the Father as the Holy Spirit works through Jesus, the Son.

A number of years ago, a friend shared a powerful analogy capturing the dynamic meaning of humility. My friend Grey compared meekness to a well-trained horse that was taught how to perform in battle. This animal was so disciplined that in the midst of a battle with all the chaos, confusion, screaming, and mayhem, this horse would remain absolutely still as it waited patiently for its rider to direct it. Can you imagine living your life in such a way? The world around you may be in total chaos and confusion, but you don't panic! Deep down in your soul, you are at peace because your faith and training informs you that your Lord is in control. We can cast off all fear, doubt, and anxiety. Through this analogy, our paradox is revealed—and we find another way to live our lives if we choose. And we can embrace Jesus' words without hesitation: "Blessed are the humble for they will inherit the earth."

Moving into the fourth principle of the kingdom, we must acknowledge a simple principle. Righteousness is one of the most difficult principles to live out. For the orthodox Jew in the time of Christ, this meant keeping the law. This required strict obedience to more than three hundred codes and biblical mandates. To live the righteous life, one did not have the option to pick and choose which laws to obey and which ones to ignore.

To break one law was to break all the laws of God; there could not be any distinction. Consequently, righteousness was beyond the grasp of people. The result was problematic because the law of God was believed to bring life itself. This idea is clearly the message that the Psalmist sought to establish in the poetic words of Psalm 119. This Psalm is the longest and seeks to define the importance of sacred law that puts you in the right relationship with God.

Anyone who has lived the human experience knows that we will always fall short of righteousness. St. Paul correctly said, "All have sinned and fall short of the glory of God" (Rom. 3:23). Paul, however, moves us past this cold reality by sharing the Good News. Our righteousness is achieved not by the law—but by faith through Jesus Christ. His sacrifice on the cross delivers us from our sin and restores our relationship with God.

At best, righteous works reflect our faith and a relationship in Christ, but they count for nothing in the general scheme of redemption. True righteousness, therefore, comes from God and all who hold his Son within their loving embrace. This precious gift is open to all Jews and Gentiles. This teaching was a profoundly radical teaching for its time. Many Hebrews could not accept it because it went against everything they had learned since childhood. Once again, the lesson opens our eyes to the mysterious world of paradox.

The teaching on righteousness was controversial for its time, but such a teaching could not be understood without considering the light of God's mercy. Mercy is the fifth principle of blessing. Mercy marks the emergence of divine compassion breaking into the reality of human brokenness. God's mercy, however, has always played a role in human redemption— beginning with the fall in the Garden of Eden and continuing to this day.

The principle act of divine mercy is found in the life, teaching, suffering, and sacrifice of Jesus the Christ and is the next principle. Throughout his earthly ministry, mercy was a driving force behind those precious moments when he healed the sick, when he gave sight to the blind, when he opened the ears of the deaf, gave mobility to the cripple, or forgave the sins of those who were ensnared in sin's bondage.

The most significant act of mercy was when he raised the dead to new life. It is important to understand that these astonishing miracles were not individual acts of redemption. As noted in John's gospel, these acts of mercy were signs that point to a greater reality. In his gospel, John only records seven miracle stories. He makes it a point not to call them "miracles." Rather, he sees these acts as signs. Each of the seven signs signifies what God is doing through his Son. From the wedding at Cana to the raising of Lazarus, John conveys a progressive story of redemption.

In his final and concluding sign, raising Lazarus from the dead, he is pointing the reader to God's work of restoring all humanity to a state of wholeness and renewal. God, through his Son and Holy Spirit, reaches out and hears the cries of his people and enters the drama of redemption.

Furthermore, God's reaching out to humankind is not a one-time act at a given point in history. God's mercy is an ongoing process to bring blessing upon blessing in one's daily life from one generation to the next. God, through the Christ, will open the eyes of the blind to see the truth; he heals those who are crippled in spirit. He touches the ears of those who are deaf and opens them to hear the word of truth. He feeds us with the bread of life to sustain us on our journeys.

God, in Christ, watches over us and provides his protection like a shepherd watching over his sheep. He therefore becomes the door to the kingdom through which we pass. And finally, like Lazarus, he raises us from the dead! This act of resurrection is a present reality that has future implications. If we live the resurrected life daily, what will we have to fear? Furthermore, in his compassion and mercy, he marks us as his own and identifies us as children of God. As his children, we are entitled—by adoption—to be heirs of the kingdom.

In the sixth principle, we are introduced to the importance of peacemakers. Peacemakers are an interesting subject in the Old Testament and are controversial in nature. For instance, many Christians are confused and perplexed as they read about the God of Israel in the Hebrew Scriptures. The confusion surfaces when they read about all the violence and destruction that is waged in the name of religion and God. Given this horrific history, some readers raise the question: "Where is the God of love, mercy, and compassion?"

Certainly, love was not the order for the day as Israel encountered her enemies. When the Israelites crossed over the Jordan River, they did not carry flowers, but swords, spears, and shields. If they were going to take possession of the land, they had to conquer its inhabitants. The Israelites were given the land based on God's covenant with Abraham (Ex. 12:1–3). No one, however, told the Canaanites, Pizzites, Hittites, Kenites, Amorites, and the rest of the people who had settled in the region that we now know as Israel. Consequently, those early wandering Hebrews had to fight for the land that was given to them by God.

More than that, we are shocked to read that they were instructed by God to drive out all the people in their conquest (Ex. 23:31–33). The land was to be purified, and all the tribes that inhabited this region had to be removed or killed. So, as Israel entered the land, she began committing genocide as a means to purify God's gift to her.

The exploits of King David, the great warrior, takes this violence to an even higher level. King David thus becomes the greatest king in Jewish history. Through his lineage, even with blood on his hands, he establishes the family line from which the Christ will come. Strangely, when this land is finally conquered, King David believes it is time to build a temple for his God, but God forbids him to do that because there is too much blood he has spilled. (1 Sam. 7:12f). Too much blood? Wasn't he doing God's will? David's actions call us to question whether or not Israel got it right when she entered the land and began the slaughter. This topic raises all sorts of theological and ethical questions that go far beyond the scope of this chapter.

This strange story once again takes us to the mystery of paradox. How could Israel claim to be doing God's will and become the means by which she also was to draw all nations to her God? How could she become a symbol of the peacemaker with such a questionable history of violence? How could she be an icon of God's love, mercy, and compassion? In raising these questions, we are not intending to disparage the early Hebrews; this thought highlights the complexity of biblical interpretation and the mystery of paradox that veils our biblical history. Throughout Israel's early development, violence was an accepted act of survival. Consequently, it came as a surprise when Jesus was calling forth peacemakers instead of warriors.

With this brief introduction, we can perhaps see why the sixth beatitude did not make sense to the Hebrews in the time of Christ. Looking back to the first century, the people of Israel were looking forward to revolting against Roman occupation, and all they needed was a Messiah who would lead them into war! Without question, it must have been a shock when Jesus announced, "Blessed are the peacemakers." What was so blessed about being a peacemaker?

First, we need to know that the word peace, "shalom" in the Hebrew, means more than the absence of war or chaos. The significance of peace is far deeper and more profound than this simple definition. In shaping a New Testament definition, Jesus and Scripture were to point out that peace is the act of growing into maturity and spiritual wholeness. In doing so, a new relationship begins to emerge between God and humankind—and between all the peoples of the world and the creation itself. Furthermore, we move into a sense of wholeness as we understand who we are, why we were created, and God's demand on our lives.

Using peacemakers, God weaves a beautiful tapestry that unites his creation. When each part is connected and plays its rightful role, we join in the process of becoming co-creators and open the doors to blessing. In this plan of divine intent, we become sons and daughters of God—not by our will, but through the acts of the Spirit of God. We can extrapolate that peacemakers are those who seek to bring others to a sense of wholeness and unity.

Peacemakers don't beat people into submission; they offer unconditional love. They love as Christ loved us. This process begins when these peacemakers help us see our brokenness, our hurts, pains, and doubts, and help us understand that we are in desperate need of a Savior. These peacemakers take us to the doorstep of God, where we are left standing, having to make a choice to enter and begin a personal relationship with Him.

When we find God, a peacemaker can gently guide us to find ourselves. In finding ourselves, we discover the mysterious state of union that exists between our body, soul, and spirit. Even more wonderful, we can accept who we are, understanding that we are created in the image of God and are like God who works in unity with the Spirit and Son. Unity creates the reality of peace.

With our newfound revelation and wisdom, we discover that we are all connected. We are connected to our past and to each other—no matter where we live on this planet. The world has become a village, and we each contribute to sustain her life. Unity becomes a building block, a cornerstone upon which the creation is established. How can we ignore the principle of unity, and its influence on our lives and the world in which we live? To turn away from this principle, is to become self-destructive. Blessed are the peacemakers for they reveal that peace is always elusive until we learn the value of unity as revealed in the work of the Holy Trinity.

The final contrarian beatitude illuminated by the Christ takes us to the value of persecution. Blessed are you who are persecuted! We can surmise that this teaching once again catches his audience off guard, especially the poor, the outcast, and those who suffered injustice at the hands of the Romans and the Jewish elite. Surely, this is a strange paradox that opens the doors to a plethora of questions.

How can we find blessings while being the object of persecution? We find no pleasure in being victims of suffering, tyranny, poverty, false imprisonment, torture, or death. Yet, when we read the sacred stories in our Judean/Christian history, we discover a cloud of witnesses who endured hardship and death for the sake of the faith. The prophets were martyred; all of the disciples of Jesus except John were tortured and killed in gruesome deaths. Even Jesus was hung on a cross, the ultimate disgrace. What can we learn from such acts of courage?

The Christian life is one that often makes us stand apart from culture. As a result, we can easily become the target of those who see our beliefs as different or threatening. We become a threat because there is something in human behavior that does not allow us to accept those who are different from the dominant culture. These differences can be physical, such as a disfiguring handicap, they can be a gender issue, or they can relate to one's ethnic makeup.

When we view people as different, we use them as our scapegoats. Think back to your youth and the playground where you spent many joyful hours. Do you remember that one kid who sometimes stood out? This was the kid who had few friends. He or she was a loner because this child may have been impeccably perfect and smart! When you first talked to this person, you may have learned that this child talked differently and had strong moral and ethical values. He or she never broke the rules and was above reproach. Worse yet, this child could not compete because of a lack of physical skills. This child was never much fun because he or she never would do anything risky or be a little mischievous; therefore, we could not trust this child.

Consequently, kids that were different were out of the loop, teased, and harassed. We singled them out at times to take the pressure off ourselves and our own shortcomings and to point our fingers at these solitary souls and persecute them.

What takes place on the playground is acted out every day throughout the adult world. In doing these same kinds of things, we fail to see the importance of the lesson such outcasts can teach their peers.

Each and every one of us must stand for what is good, right, and honorable as if these values have been stamped into our DNA. How we live our lives has immeasurable value to ourselves and the societies that nurture our development. Without these values, our homes, villages, and nations will unravel. Therefore, it behooves each of us to live our lives beyond reproach and to stand up for the values that sustain life and our belief system that is rooted in truth. Yes, this means we will sometimes be marked for suffering and persecution.

We suffer because our values become a threat to the dominant group, system, or culture. Jesus acknowledges this reality when he shares with his disciples that they too will suffer and be persecuted because of him (Mark 8:34–37). And we take note that there is more to life than what we can see, hear, or feel. What we believe and stand up for builds a legacy for ourselves, our families, and those who come after us. In essence, some things are so precious that they are worth dying for because they offer a gift of immeasurable value.

When persecuted, we must be willing to make the sacrifice to preserve that which gives eternal life. Jesus said, "Greater love has no one than this, that one lay down his life for his friends. You are my friends if you do what I command" (John 15:13–14).

In sacrificing himself for us, Jesus underscores the value of his life, teaching, and ministry—and the truth upon which it is grounded. Had he not died for us, could we ever fully grasp the profound nature of the gift he has given us? He died for what he believed. He believed in his Father, and he believes in you. How do we know? No one ever dies for a lie or that which does not offer truth. When someone suffers and gives up his life for our sake, it can only mean one thing—the extent to which we are loved.

The Sermon on the Mount continues to be one of the most profound teachings in the Scriptures. Jesus' words have withstood the test of time. Yet, when he offered them, it was a contrarian world view. Many Hebrews could not accept his words because his teaching totally contradicted the world as they understood it. What he offered was a paradox.

His paradox, however, does not leave us in darkness and confusion. He guides us out of the weeds; with each step, he illumines our journey in order to understand the will of his Father.

Chapter Two

WHEAT OR WEEDS?

EVERY day, when you wake up to the glory of the rising sun, you never know if you are going to be standing amidst the wheat or the weeds. Each day holds a new surprise, and only time and God will help you unwrap that which remains hidden. As we watch the day unfold, every moment of the day will open us to a countless number of blessings. However, in an instant, we can find ourselves cursed by darkness. When we are subject to the latter, we watch the world around us crumble under our feet. We are stunned and dazed—and we are often left wondering how something that is so right ends up being so wrong. This strange twist of fate is even more troubling when we think we are basking in the glory of God's grace and acting according to his will. Such was the case one bright, sunny winter morning on the high plains of Laramie, Wyoming.

On the morning in question, I had a surprise visit from my daughter Andrina. A sophomore at the University of Wyoming, she showed great potential in her academic pursuits. She was a young woman of striking beauty, talented, and intelligent. As a proud father, I watched her progress at UW with eager expectations to see how this young flower would blossom and capture the attention of the world around her.

In her quest to discover her calling, she had explored creative writing and art classrooms where men and women developed their creative abilities in the fine arts. Whichever way she turned, I knew that she would be successful. How could she not be? Many of us accept the perceived reality that the young, the beautiful, and the talented people of our world always achieve the goals that are set before them. We have it in our minds that the beautiful people of our culture are always destined to succeed. Are they not? At least this is the cultural myth that many of us assume as truth.

When my lovely daughter cornered me in the living room and said, "Dad, we need to talk," I was not alarmed. I thought that her statement was benign and could not be a serious problem. Perhaps she was having a problem with a boyfriend or an issue with one of her professors. Maybe it was a relationship problem with one of her roommates. How serious could it be? How much trouble could a twenty-year-old get into when she was living a couple of blocks away under the watchful eye of her parents? We were prepared to allow her to explore her independence in her own apartment, but nothing could prepare me for the conversation that followed—and changed the course of all of our lives.

Andrina began by saying that some strange things were beginning to happen to her. *What could be so strange that prompted this conversation?* She began to tell me about an event that had taken place a couple of nights earlier. She had been alone at her apartment. All of a sudden, she got a strange urge to step outside and onto the balcony. From there, she could not resist the compulsion to step up onto the rail of the balcony. As she stood there, delicately keeping her balance on the balcony railing, a voice deep within her told her to step off and fly. A cold chill went down my spine because she lived on the third level of the apartment building; had she listened to that voice and taken that step, I doubted if we would be having that conversation.

She continued, having grabbed my full attention, explaining that she was hearing these voices with alarming frequency. I quickly tried to dismiss the conversation, thinking that this young woman was merely exploring another side to her personality—nothing more. I was in denial, and I was already trying to diminish the seriousness of our discussion.

As we continued our talk, I quickly assessed that my daughter was serious. She was calling out for help. I could see it in her eyes and tell from her voice that these experiences were troubling. Uncharacteristically, she asked if she could see a counselor. I agreed that this would be our next step. I was thinking that she could enter counseling; after a couple of sessions, she would clear her head, and we could both return to normalcy. However, this thought soon would be swept away as if it were scooped up by the high plains winds.

Shortly after our conversation, we arranged for Andrina to see one of my staff members. At the time, I was dean of St. Matthew's Cathedral. The cathedral is the central church for the Episcopal Diocese of Wyoming, and I was the priest in charge. Fortunately, I had a practicing psychologist on staff. He, too, was ordained in the Episcopal Church, but his primary vocation was working in the mental health arena.

When I called to set up the appointment, I explained the situation and the conversation Andrina had shared with me. He immediately put her on his calendar. Within days, she was in his office sitting before him and telling him this strange tale. After a couple of sessions, our psychologist called us all in for a meeting. The news was not good. He explained that Andrina was indeed having some serious mental health issues. Then he hit us with a bombshell!

When he told us that she appeared to be suffering from schizophrenia with paranoid tendencies, his words crushed my soul! I was stunned! I questioned how this could happen. Although those words sent chills down my spine, I clutched my denial as if it offered a glimmer of hope. My associate added some pressure when he suggested referring her to a psychiatrist for further evaluation. He had established his diagnosis, but before going any further, we needed to get a second opinion.

His statement allowed me to grasp my denial for a little longer. Nevertheless, I felt as if I were standing under a large black Wyoming thunderhead that was about to burst and release a torrent of rain, lightning, and thunder. Looking into the eyes of my colleague, there was no hiding the look of concern on his face.

Since Laramie was in short supply of psychiatrists—and wanting only the best care for our daughter—we began to search in the Denver area. With help from our church's national headquarters, we got a referral for a doctor in Fort Collins, Colorado, which was a little over an hour away. Finding the right person, however, would be problematic. Andrina was extremely sensitive regarding with whom she would share her deepest and darkest secrets. She was already suffering from paranoia; we had to be careful. If she did not connect with this person, she might judge all psychiatrists alike and refuse further diagnosis and treatment. To assure her, I told her I would be right at her side. In addition, if this doctor did not work out, then we would find one with whom she felt more comfortable.

The drive to Fort Collins from Laramie on Highway 287 is scenic, especially near the border of Colorado. As you drive south and cross the border, you are welcomed by a forest of ponderosa pine trees; off to the west, the Snowy Range Mountains rise in magnificent glory. If you are lucky, sometimes you can catch a herd of elk grazing peacefully off the road.

However, this was not one of those peaceful trips. Andrina and I were filled with anxiety about the uncertain future. We drove in silence; both of us were caught up in our own private thoughts. It was a long drive. When we arrived in Fort Collins, we easily found the doctor's office on the main street.

The office was clean, well-furnished, and decorated with tasteful modern art. It was a safe and pleasant setting that looked out a large window toward a peaceful pond. After filling out the necessary paperwork, we were invited into the doctor's office. He was a tall, middle-aged man with a gentle face and a reassuring voice. His presence was welcoming, and with his silver hair, he reflected experience and wisdom.

After the brief introductions and a warm-up conversation, he began to probe Andrina with questions to gently reveal her issues. I liked his bedside manner, and Andrina seemed comfortable as she responded to his questions. With each question, I began to see for myself the troubled world that my daughter was trying to conceal from her mother and me. I could not imagine this world as she knew it. She revealed strange voices whispering softly to her as if she were in the presence of ghosts who were trying to manipulate her world. To make matters worse, she was seeing spiders crawl out of the walls.

She talked about having conversations with people. As they talked, she would watch in horror as their faces melted and distorted! If their faces were not melting, then the words she heard were troubling. In her psychotic state, she would hear people tell her that she was a "bitch" or she was "ugly" and other phrases that were much more troubling. With these episodes, I could see that she was losing touch with reality. With each session, I became more and more aware of the frightful world that was consuming her soul.

Until that point in my life and ministry, I had little contact with the mentally ill. Sure, I had members of my parish who had reported that a close relative had been recently diagnosed with a mental illness. Then there was the occasional homeless person who would wander into the church seeking assistance, but I never sought to draw them into my presence. Since they were in transit from one town to another, I did not know how to address their needs! Worse, I could not relate to their perception of reality. Therefore, much like the rest of society, I gave them what they needed for the moment and sent them on their way.

My own daughter was trying to survive in a living hell, and I did not know what to do or how to help. The only thing I could possibly accomplish was to get her connected with a mental health caregiver and learn as much as possible about this disease. Nevertheless, I soon sank into my own world of depression. Worse, I did not seek help. How could I? I was supposed to be a healer.

Over the next few months, in the quiet moments of my own thoughts, I wrestled with her diagnosis. Andrina was the child who was blessed, and now she appeared to be cursed. A question continued to surface that I could not resolve: "What did she do to deserve this?" Her illness was a large stone hanging from her neck, and she would have to carry it for the rest of her life. With this question still looming in the air, I wondered about her future. Would she marry? Would she have her own children? Would she forge a life for herself that would fulfill her wants and needs?

I was haunted with the thought that she was a beautiful person, and tragedies like this do not happen to the beautiful people. Most troubling, I felt betrayed by God! This betrayal was something of which I never spoke—not even to my wife. These thoughts and feelings were my secret. Nevertheless, like any parent, deep down inside, I wondered why this was happening. I even made the mistake of searching my soul for some dark sin for which my daughter and I must now pay the price.

Previously, I had categorized such thoughts as poor theology. Sure, the Hebrew Bible says that the sins of the father will be passed on to the son to the second and third generations (2 Sam. 7:14). There may well be some truth to this statement—but only as a general statement.

I have long observed that we pass on to our children many dysfunctional behaviors that prevent us from being the people God has called us to be. Why? Children will often repeat what they see and hear. The consequences of what we do and how we live our lives are oftentimes played out in the lives of our children. They repeat the habits and actions that we consciously or unconsciously establish in our families of origin.

With more than twenty-four years of ministry—and having become a student of human behavior—I have come to believe that we can, through our DNA, pass on more than our eye color or our skin tone, body type, or physical ability. In the years to come, science may prove that our genetic makeup is a vault of family history, illness, and characteristics that exposes us to events that date back generations and predispose us to our future.

What can we say about our sin? Can our children be punished for the sins of their parents or grandparents? In the Hebrew Scriptures, this question is answered with a definitive yes. If you believe in the sin of Adam (original sin), sin is alive and well as it casts its dark shadow over all humanity. Today, there are many in the Christian community who would challenge this premise. This question lives in the arena of debate, but the fact remains that there are no easy answers. This being the case, I was left struggling with my daughter's illness. In the face of my denial and depression, I, like my daughter, could not determine fact from fiction. As a result, I carried my wounds deep within me and hid them from prying eyes.

During the following months, my wife and I began to learn as much as we could about this mental disorder. We read books and reviewed articles on the Internet. What we learned was somewhat surprising: despite this disease, some schizophrenics became doctors, artists, or counselors. We learned that some people could, with proper medical care, deal successfully with this disease. Nevertheless, nowhere did we find information calling this illness a blessing. Consequently, in our own minds, Andrina was living with a curse!

Since my days in seminary, I thought I had a good understanding of the concept of what constituted a blessing and what was a curse. Scripture seems to be quite clear. Follow God's will and you will be blessed. Deviate from his purpose and you will reap the consequences. This definition was as simple as that.

In fact, this simple doctrine of blessings and curses is built into the structure of the book of Deuteronomy. This entire book was written in the form of what was called in the ancient world the Suzerain-Vassal Treaty (NIV Study Bible, 19).

In ancient times, when a king conquered his rival nation, the king would enter into a covenant relationship. This covenant called for the absolute obedience of the conquered people. Consequently, the victor established certain laws by which the people would live. In addition, the people would swear their absolute obedience to their new king. Once these laws were established, the king outlined the blessings that would come as a result of their obedience. On the other hand, if the conquered nation became rebellious, then it would reap the curse and ire of the sovereign lord. These curses were specifically outlined in the treaty.

These treaties were quite common throughout the Middle East. Israel adopted the treaty format and made it applicable to her theology and her relationship with God. God would be Israel's king. Now, God was calling Israel into a covenant relationship with well-established laws. Therefore, it was important to note that this treaty established the idea that blessings would follow if these laws were strictly adhered to. This concept of covenant and obedience was a cornerstone to building their society. Therefore, it behooved God to set his covenant into the hearts of his people. Consequently, every seven years, the people of Israel renewed this covenant on a day of celebration. Furthermore, God instructed Moses to teach his priests the law. The priests in turn would teach the people.

This concept of obedience to the law has survived to this day. Culturally, we believe that if you follow the law and become a good person, you will be blessed. This belief, however, is shaken when some tragic event occurs. For example, take the person who has worked for a company for twenty years. He has been a loyal and dedicated employee. Therefore, he should reap the blessings of his labors and secure his future. Why should this person be laid off because of an economic downturn? Shouldn't loyalty, dedication, and sacrifice pay benefits?

We live in a world, however, where this thought is not grounded in reality; people are left wondering where the blessing is. Equally as tragic, there are those who live a healthy lifestyle—they exercise regularly, do not smoke, watch their diets—yet they end up with cancer! What about those people who are mistakenly accused of a crime? In the annals of justice, we can read horrifying stories of law-abiding citizens who were unjustly accused and convicted of a crime that they never committed. In some cases these individuals were convicted of a homicide and sentenced to death! Then, years later, they were found to be innocent due to the discovery of new evidence. Were they blessed for being good citizens? The point is simple—the lines of blessings and curses oftentimes become blurred as we deal with the complex reality of life and the world in which we live.

As Andrina entered this maze of complexity, she and I tried to understand what God was doing in her life. Andrina, however, was not alone. She is joined by a plethora of biblical witnesses who were subjected to a curse and troubling episodes in their lives. In the book of Ruth, we are reminded of her tragedy when she lost her husband (Ruth 1). In losing her husband, she lost her means of support and the promise of being blessed with the gift of children. In losing her husband, she was thrown into chaos, having to rely on the generosity of strangers.

Like Andrina, Esther was another heroic figure in Hebrew history who had to overcome a troubled past. A heroine of the Jewish nation, she saved them from slaughter and continued the lineage from which the Messiah would be born. Then there is the quintessential heroine—Mary, the mother of Jesus. Was Mary blessed among woman? Was she given a blessing at the annunciation or a curse?

The fact was that she conceived a child out of wedlock, thus subjecting her to the possibility of being stoned to death. I do not think Mary felt blessed when she had to travel from Nazareth to Bethlehem to give birth. After giving birth, was she overjoyed to learn that King Herod was out to kill her son? She and Joseph had to flee into the desert to live in exile.

Who among us would feel blessed to watch a child be subjected to an unjust trial, found guilty, and whipped and hanged from a tree? Like Jesus' disciples, Mary did not understand the blessing until that glorious Easter Sunday when she could once again hold him in her arms, kiss him on his cheek, and hear him say, "I was resurrected." All of these women of faith entered into the world of paradox and emerged with a profound understanding of God's grace.

Is there some way to understand this complex world and the biblical concept of blessings and curses? In such complexity, can we be true to our faith? Can we trust God when he calls us to follow him? Can we trust his Word that our lives will be blessed as he calls us into a personal relationship with him? Can we look into the dark shadows of our lives—or at our sons or daughters—and see a blessing in the midst of a curse?

The purpose of this book is to help those who struggle, as I did, with this concept of blessings and curses. As we enter this mysterious journey, I hope to offer insight into finding light in the midst of darkness, love in the midst of fear, and peace in the midst of confusion. All we need to know is how and where to look. Although my daughter was standing in the midst of the weeds, she would find her way back to the wheat.

Chapter 3

The Core Values of Blessings

Every parent who has had to deal with mental illness of their child knows the deep sense of grief while coming to grips with this devastating diagnosis. My wife and I were no different. When we first were told of Andrina's illness, we sank into a deep depression as reality set in. We felt alone and helpless. We could not even comfort each other because we chose not to talk about her situation or our feelings. We were walking in the weeds and not knowing any better; the best we could do was to take life a day at a time.

Most young people who are afflicted with schizophrenia must endure a painful and difficult life which often leads to isolation, homelessness, hospitalization, jail, or even suicide. Through the grace of God, however, our daughter escaped this gloomy scenario.

This is not to say she did not have tough times. There were a number of days when she sank into deep depression. During several of these episodes, her depression became so acute that she contemplated relieving her pain by ending her life. When she revealed this fact to me, I questioned why she did not reach out to her mother or me. Then she opened up my mind to a new revelation that enlightened my understanding as to why people take their own lives.

> Dad, you don't understand that when you're in such a deep depression, you can't reach out to another person. The depression consumes all rational thinking. When you cannot think rationally, you cannot comprehend the consequences of your actions. All you want is to escape your emotional pain. Consequently, you are left with no hope, and without hope, you can't see your future. If you don't have a future, there is nothing motivating you to live! You become captured in your own nightmare.

She went on to say that even the loving support of those who care about you cannot help you escape the living hell in which you find yourself.

With this insightful explanation, Andrina finally helped me understand one of the mysteries of suicide. Strangely, her words brought a sense of comfort because years before, a close friend of mine took his own life after losing his job and separating from his wife and children. His response to his crisis was to start drinking again to dull the pain. His drinking sent him spiraling into the depths of despair. Within a short time, he reached rock bottom, and he ended it all.

For years, I grieved his death as I tried to answer the "what-if questions" that haunted my memories. I was troubled because I was not able to be of help to him. Now, my daughter provided the answer. When someone finds themselves in this black hole, there is nothing one can do—especially when the person separates from family and friends. The best that we have to offer is our unconditional love and support. More importantly, we need to recognize the signs of self- destruction and get these individuals into a mental health treatment center. There, mental health professionals can start addressing the chemical imbalance that often precedes this mental condition while also focusing on the life situations that are leading to this harmful decision.

Not fully understanding his desperate situation, I was mad at my friend for years for making that final exit! I was angry because he was not willing to give himself a second chance and turn around his misfortune. He was not willing to turn to me as his friend. He could not understand that suicide is never the final solution. There are countless people who can testify that suicide is a temporary state of mind—and that there is life beyond the thoughts of self-destruction.

From a rational standpoint, it is extremely difficult to understand why someone would take this drastic plunge. Thankfully, my daughter was already under the treatment of a mental health caregiver. Through antidepressants and therapy, she was able to survive those black, challenging months when she was living in a world of hallucinations and mysterious voices.

Nevertheless, something began to happen; it was her own little miracle. She started searching for the blessings in the midst of her weeds. The wheat and the weeds were growing side by side; she just needed to recognize which one was which. So, she began to look more closely at her life.

In her exploration process, she came to terms with the fact that she had been shallow and selfish.

In response to her understanding of self, she began to learn humility. Her humility opened her heart to be more empathetic toward those individuals who, like her, had been cast out to the fringes of our society. Her disease helped her to see living a life that was simpler. Her disease taught her that we grow up in world of blessings and curses; if we are patient, we can identify the wheat from the weeds. So despite all of our fears, our daughter was able to overcome each obstacle that was placed in her path and move on.

That which Andrina learned over the course of her mental illness, St. Paul also learned over the course of his life. He wrote a rather profound observation in great boldness in his letter to the Ephesians. He said, "Always give thanks for all things in the name of the Lord Jesus Christ" (Eph. 5:20). Such statements cause us to pause and think. Can we thank God for all things? Could I thank God for my daughter's mental condition? Could I thank God for the countless poor choices I had made in my life as I planted the weeds in my field? Can we thank God when those two planes crashed into the World Trade Center or when a wall of water overwhelmed towns and villages in northern Japan? Rationally, our thoughts and feelings say no!

The Scriptures, however, persuade us to reframe the question in the world of paradox.

We can learn to thank God for all things, but we will first need to understand what I call the core values of blessings. These core values open a world that is unfamiliar to some and avoided by others. Take heed; when we enter the veil of avoidance, we run the risk of repeating the same mistakes. Our healing and wholeness become elusive, and we may find ourselves standing in the weeds for years. We must take further note: there are no shortcuts or easy paths on the road to blessing. Many times, we must wait.

In waiting, however, we do not wait idly. We wait with probing eyes to see the wonders of God's kingdom unfold before us. We must remember that Jesus taught us about the interconnecting values of blessing and kingdom. In essence, the kingdom, God's rule in our lives, unfolds when we discover the secret—the core values of blessing. Where do we find these core values? These core values are strung throughout the Hebrew and Christian Scriptures in the pages of sacred stories of countless seekers. In their journeys, they discovered the light that marks the way to wisdom, revelation, and illumination.

We must keep in mind that core values are not the sole claim of the Judeo-Christian heritage; these values belong to all who seek to draw closer to our creator. We must first accept the reality that God reveals himself in all of his creation—and even in the writings of other wisdom literature whose authors have come face to face with truth. Ultimately, if Jesus is who he claims to be, if the resurrection is a reality, then Christianity holds a unique position in its proclamations of truth. So, we will explore the Scriptures as they speak to this truth. In doing so, we will uncover the seven core values of blessing.

First, in reading these sacred stories, we learn quickly that a blessing is conveyed through the power of the spoken word. According to *The New International Dictionary of New Testament Thought,* Vol. 1, a blessing is a promise given by one in authority and whose words impart a benefit or power. In addition, this promise is unconditional and irrevocable (Brown, 206–218).

Looking at the Hebrew Scriptures, we clearly observe this definition in the story of Jacob when he steals his father's blessing from his older brother Esau (Gen. 27:30f). This ancient biblical blessing was always reserved for the oldest male in the family, and it was given to pass on power and good fortune. Esau, however, sells his birthright to his younger brother for a little food! When Esau comes to his senses and realizes that he sold off his birthright, he goes to his father to plead for another blessing, but it is too late! His father only had one blessing to give. That blessing had already rolled off his lips and found its way to his younger brother, Jacob, and those words of blessing could not be retracted.

To us moderns, we may think that such blessings were just part of the ancient folklore that has no real impact on our lives. In *The Blessing,* Dr. John Trent makes a powerful argument to the contrary. Trent points out that a fatherly blessing is a critical component to the emotional, social, and spiritual development of his children. Trent sees the gift of blessing as the power to develop and strengthen the masculinity or femininity of our offspring. When a father offers his blessing, his most precious words build character and allow his children to move into the world with confidence. Confidence grows and develops because these children are secure, knowing that they have the unconditional loving support from family. With this love, children can move out of their comfort zone; they are free to explore and even take risks, knowing that their parents are always in close proximity to offer a safety net in case they stumble. Consequently, Trent astutely articulates that a blessing will define a favorable future to its recipient.

Tragically, in our society "the blessing" is held beyond the reach of some children especially in dysfunctional households. The results are foreboding. If the blessing has been withheld, children will look for love and acceptance in unhealthy places, usually among their peers. Their desire for love, acceptance, and affirmation is so strong that if they do not receive this blessing in a positive environment, they will turn to a negative one. As a result, they may find themselves lost in a weed patch.

Not only are blessings offered through the spoken word, these words of love and affirmation were expected to be offered frequently. In *The Path of Blessing*, Rabbi Prager informs us that within every Jewish household, it was expected that a blessing be offered at least one hundred times a day! Such a demand was to awaken in each person a god-consciousness and the wondrous glory and awe of his creation and presences. With this river of praise, a blessing was not offering just words—more importantly, it was a lifestyle. The ancient Hebrews understood that their whole life was to be lived as a blessing from God; each moment, everyday people were called to recognize the divine presence and to lift their voices in praise (Prager, 42). The power of seeing and extending blessings forces us to stop, to look, and to listen to the miracles—big and small—that await our discovery with the dawning of each new day, the passing of each hour, and the sweeping of every second.

Can you begin to imagine what life would look like as we discover the words of blessing? We would awaken our consciousness to the fact that words have power. The words of blessing have the power to heal, restore, build up, correct, forgive, reveal truth, and give life! Throughout the Scriptures, we see God offering these words of blessing.

The second core value of blessing is seen in the characteristic of a humble spirit. This should not be a new revelation; humility is always a valued quality in pursuit of wisdom and the kingdom. In *Summa Theologica*, Thomas Aquinas captures this thought. He said, "Humility frees and disposes us to receive God's blessing." Aquinas understood the importance of the open spirit that allows us to move outside our own narrow thinking and gaze with wonder at God's creation from a different perspective. Such truth is experienced every day in our lives.

Think for a moment and place yourself at the north edge of the Grand Canyon in the early morning. As you look out over the desert, the sun begins to illumine the desert before you. Then, you turn around one-hundred-and-eighty degrees, and as the sun rises further, it illumines the canyon below. You gasp at the myriad colors and the awesomeness of the creation. You are standing at the same position—all you have done is change your focal point—and a miracle of nature is revealed as this wondrous vision takes your breath away. This simple illustration helps us to grasp the nature of a humble spirit.

A humble spirit is one that can take directions and change its focal point as it opens itself to a new perspective. The blessing is discovered by looking at your life and the world around you from a new vantage point and being molded like a piece of clay. We, however, are not the potter. Humility is not developed. Humility is a sign of something far more important that is going on in the individual.

In Vol. 2 of *The New International Dictionary of New Testament Theology,* we see an insightful observation that humility shows that a person is taking on the very image of Christ. Humility, therefore, is a sign revealing that those who clothe themselves with it are souls who have been called into relationship with God; their humility is sign of this fact. Furthermore, humility is an outward sign of salvation. Salvation in this respect is a present reality that we experience now and not as a future hope (Bailey, 257).

Jesus captures this concept in the teaching of the beatitudes. He declares, "Blessed are the meek for they shall inherit the kingdom of God" (Matt. 5:5). The biblical words "meek" and "humble" are used almost synonymously. Both words describe a person who is a tower of strength! In our culture, we think of someone who is meek as a person who lacks conviction, strength, or courage. Consequently, to be called a meek person is not very complimentary, and we would probably take offense at the suggestion! This definition is far from the mind of Christ.

In his teaching of the beatitudes, the meek are those believers who have built a character of obedience, discipline, courage, and faith. The result is that nothing that takes place in their lives can affect them negatively because they trust that God will work all things out and they are connected to the head of the Church, Jesus Christ.

When someone separates himself from Christ, the consequences can be profound. Separation causes paralysis and does not allow one to fully function. Such was the case with our dog Falstaff. Falstaff was a little terrier. One day we went to town and left him outside to his own devices. When we arrived home, we found him on the front porch. Upon seeing us he began to move the front part of his body with excitement. Something, however, was terribly wrong. He could not move his back legs. We rushed him to the veterinarian only to discover that he had either been hit by a car or involved in a fight with a large dog. The consequences were severe. His brain was giving him signals to walk, but because the nerves were severed, his back legs could not receive the signals. Falstaff was paralyzed. He could not receive directions from his head.

What happened to Falstaff became a living metaphor. His condition was a picture of what happens when people lose their connection to the author of life, Jesus the Christ. Whether it be pride, stubbornness, obstinacy, or rebellion, they do not open themselves to the living Lord. As a result, they are living in paralysis. Humility brings us to the third core value of blessing: patience. In the parable of the wheat and weeds, Jesus implies that patience is an essential element of illumination and discovery. Over the centuries, Christians have elevated patience as one of the founding principles of faith.

St. John Avila, when writing to his students, shares this thought: "Patience is the guardian of all the other virtues, and, if it fails, we may lose in one moment the labor of many days (*The Quotable Saints,* 195).

Cyprian of Carthage takes our understanding one step further. "Patient waiting is necessary that we may have begun to be, and through God's help, that we may obtain what we hope for and believe" (*The Quotable Saints,* 195).

When we embrace patience and live by its rule, we take on a God-like quality that allows all things to take their course in due time. We, therefore, do not acknowledge our timetable, but work in God's time. One who studies the nature of creation recognizes that patience is revealed in the evolutionary process of our world. Our creation is a work of time; the Grand Canyon is an example.

In essence, patience gives us the precious gift of time—time to adapt, time to reflect, time to grow in wisdom, time to pray, time to be transformed, and time to enter into the right moment that puts us in synchronization with God's time. As seconds turn to minutes, minutes to hours, and hours into days, these movements can change how we see God working in the situations of our lives. During these epiphanies, we may be surprised to find ourselves saying, "Oh! Now, I understand."

In the world of biblical thought, there are two types of time. Time can be measured by the passing of the chronological ticking of the minutes. The second is allowing the passage of time, waiting with eager expectation to enter into God's perfect time. In God's time, one can enter into the right moment when life's energies converge, thus allowing God's design to unfold. Understanding this important concept moves us past waiting anxiously to a calm state of mind and ultimately into a state of peace.

Our patience takes us to the doorstep of the fifth core value of blessing: thankfulness. In both the Judeo and Christian traditions, thankfulness opens the door that allows us to stand in awe and wonder as we gaze upon the creative spirit in us and around us. We see that through God's grace, nothing is lost—and nothing is wasted.

Faustina Kowalska captures this thought in one of her writings.

> My spirit engrossed itself in the benefits
> that God has lavished on me throughout

the whole year. My soul trembled at the sight of the immensity of God's grace. From my soul burst forth a hymn of thanksgiving to the Lord. For a whole hour, I remained steeped in adoration and thanksgiving, contemplation, one by one the benefits I had received from God and my own shortcomings. All that this year contained has gone in the abyss of eternity. Nothing is lost. I am glad nothing gets lost. (*The Quotable Saints*, 274)

After reading this thoughtful piece, I began to search my own soul, wondering when my soul trembled in delight at the sight of God's blessings. When did my soul call out with unaccountable joy? When did I celebrate my shortcomings, recognizing that there are latent blessings in my shortcomings? In fact, joy and thanksgiving are made more efficacious as we see God working through our weaknesses and faults. In essence, thanksgiving is more than an action word of offering praise or adoration.

In both the Hebrew and Christian traditions, thanksgiving is encouraged to be a lifestyle, a constant state of being rather than random encounters. We can enter into a constant state of thanksgiving that informs and radiates within our soul because we cannot be overcome by darkness and evil.

We live in the triumphant spirit of thankfulness in all things because God has redeemed us through Christ and in Christ. We have already inherited the victory! This insight becomes the powerful proclamation of the Church's first theologian, St. Paul. St. Paul was no stranger to hardship and of recognizing his own shortcomings. He endured shipwrecks, beatings, betrayal, and imprisonments, yet the words of thanksgiving were never far from his lips.

In many of his letters, the first thing that Paul acknowledged was his thanksgiving for the saints to whom he had addressed his letter and their faithfulness to the Good News of the gospel of Christ. In his letter to the Romans, we find one of his most powerful statements on this topic. Paul reminds the church that God is working his purpose out. "And if God is working for us, who then can be against us?" (Rom. 8:31).

St. Paul presents the argument that Christ gave his life for us and it is he who justifies us before God, his Father. Moreover, Jesus is the one who continues to intercede on our behalf in our daily walk in life. With such a powerful, dynamic exhibition of love, who can deny raising his or her voice in thanksgiving and praise? Our thanksgiving greatly diminishes the power of our afflictions and claims victory over tribulation, distress, peril, and hunger. We stand as victors with him who gave his life for us. Nothing, therefore, can separate us from the love of God! But, here lies the greatest challenge of the Christian life—to be thankful for all things. Without doing so, we can never learn to understand the mysteries that unlock God's blessings for us. The Easter event is a prime example. We cannot celebrate the resurrection of Jesus until we experience the drama and pain of Good Friday.

This movement of blessing brings us to another critical and difficult example of blessing. The sixth core value of blessing has to do with letting go. Divestiture of our will, desire, and self-motivated interest removes the roadblock that divides us from God. This process of giving up does not take away our freedom of will. What we seek in this process is to open our spirit to the Spirit of God. In doing so, we become co-creators of divine will as we enter into a synergistic relationship that builds, restores, and heals our lives and the world in which we live.

When we explore the Scriptures and examine our own life experiences, we quickly discover that—more often than not—we must be willing to let go of our wants before we can discover a blessing. Think of Abraham when God calls upon him to establish a covenant of blessing. When God speaks to Abraham, Abraham is living in the land of Ur. This is his home and the home of his ancestors. This land contains all that is familiar. He has an established lifestyle, family, and friends.

When God calls upon him, Abraham has to divest himself of that which has value. He leaves behind the land of Ur. He leaves his friends and his extended family. Abram, however, is open to be directed by the Spirit of God. In his journey of discovery, he takes along his wife, Sarai, his nephew Lot, all their possessions, and "people" that they pick up along the way in Haran. God tells Abraham that if he is willing to leave behind his country, leave his father's house and relatives, and be open to the land that God will show him, then Abraham will reap the blessing.

Abraham divests himself of that which has value for him; little did he know that he had entered the drama of redemption for the human family. He is to be the father of a great nation; his name will become great and never lost in history. He will become a blessing, and his household will be a blessing to the world. His seed will ultimately become the seed from which Jesus will claim his heritage. In this covenant relationship, God blesses those who bless Abraham's household and curse those who curse them. For these events to unfold, Abraham has to let go of his past and move into the mysterious future that lies before him.

When we open the pages to the New Testament, we find that blessings often follow divestiture. In the fourth chapter of Matthew's gospel, we find the story of Jesus calling his first disciples. Matthew tells us that as Jesus was walking next to the shore of the Sea of Galilee, he encounters two brothers, Peter and Andrew, fishing. We can assume these brothers were no strangers to the Christ. They had probably heard him speak at the synagogue at Capernaum and were impressed! When they meet him by the sea and he calls them into service, they are willing to divest themselves of their occupations, their families, and their community and follow this charismatic teacher.

Soon after this encounter with Peter and Andrew, Jesus meets James and John mending their nets by the shore. Once again, the invitation goes out to leave what they are doing and follow him. In other words, leave their family, friends, and community to follow him. Now if we think that these were just poor fishermen who saw a better opportunity to leave their occupations and find an easier life, we have to think again.

Zebedee, their father, was the owner of the boat. He had established a family business. Though not rich, this business provided a good income—enough to support multiple families. Therefore, when Jesus called upon these men, he was asking them to leave behind their security and enter a journey that led them down an unknown road. They had to let go in order to find their way to the blessings before them.

Now, think about your own life. Think specifically about the blessings you have encountered in your life. How did those blessing unfold? What did you have to let go of before you could see God's gracious hand at work as he molded your sacrifice into an unexpected blessing?

We have all come to know that those things that mean the most in our lives require a sacrifice on our part. Many times, we have to give up something. We divest ourselves of desires, and we are willing to pay a price to achieve that which offers a greater good. In our willingness to let go of the past or that which lays claim on our lives, we must even let go of those situations and persons who have hurt us. We are then able to look at life from a different perspective that gives us greater insight. In letting go, we need to recognize that we do not have all the answers to the questions that haunt and obstruct our lives. To let go, we must acquire the ability to listen tentatively to the voice of the Spirit of God. If not, our closed spirit can—and will—impede our ability to grasp God's abundant outreach.

Living in abundance brings us to the fourth core value of blessing: love. I am not speaking of love as an emotion but as an action. Love as an action is how God defines love. God's love is demonstrated by his acts of mercy, compassion, forgiveness, healing, and his willingness to enter into the lives of a broken people. Jesus Christ personifies this concept as we read about his ministry in the Gospels. Everything he does—every word he offers—is designed to show his Father's love.

Ultimately, Jesus demonstrates his love for us by his sacrificial act in stretching out his arms of love on the cross. The love of God offered on a cross two thousand years ago was not a single act. Many of the actions we take have a limited effect. Christ's act of love continues to change lives and shape our unfolding history. This powerful act of love can overcome any other power or authority on earth.

Love, therefore, becomes the cornerstone of blessing; without it, nothing can stand alone. Without love, words have no lasting value. Without love, patience gives way to time. Without love, truth can be distorted. Without love, humility can soon become self-serving. Without love, we lose our connection to self, others, and our creator.

Theresa of Lisrewcex in "The Story of the Soul" in *The Quotable Saints,* brings us to one of the important aspects of love.

> You know, God, that I have never wanted anything but to love you and you alone. Your love has gone before me from my childhood, it has grown with me, and now it is an abyss whose depths I cannot plummet. Love attracts love and wipes sorrows up to you, eager to fill the abyss of your love, but not even a drop of dew is lost in the ocean. To love you as you love me, I must borrow your love and only then can I have peace. (Guiley, 157)

Theresa graciously reminds us that love attracts love as if it were a magnet. Love cannot deny its own true nature. Love that is shared has a synergy that cannot be denied; its whole is greater than its parts and continually grows in its power to transform our lives and those with whom we share our lives. As described by Teresa of Lisrewcex, we come to the final value of love. Our love for God—and God's love for us—fills us with blessings that bring us peace.

Love and peace bring us to the last core value of blessing: sharing. When God bestows upon us a blessing, his blessing is not intended for us alone. Blessings are always intended to infuse the creation with the energy of God. Blessings can—and should— be a dynamic force that has a mystical way of growing and building up the world in which we live.

By its very nature, a blessing offered cries out within our soul to be shared. Think for a moment of the last time you received God's blessing. How did you feel? Was your joy bubbling over? Did you feel that you would burst if you did not share that joy with another person! When this happens, the natural tendency for each of us is to confront this compulsion and to share the good news by which you were empowered. Too often, we stop at this point and never think that when we are empowered by a blessing, we are called upon to empower others. It is in this marvelous movement of spirit that we become co-creators with God.

In sharing the blessing, we give hope, build faith, establish a future, and enrich the lives of others. In doing so, the blessing returns to us tenfold and it renews us upon its return. Just as importantly, sharing a blessing gives us unity of purpose as we seek to be instruments of God's grace.

We see this sacred movement as we read the history of the early Hebrews when God establishes his convenient and promises them their own land through the Abrahamic Covenant. In giving these nomadic people a land flowing with milk and honey, this blessing is not a gift just for the twelve tribes of Israel. When God blesses them, it is his purpose to show the rest of the world how gracious and awesome Israel's God is. In doing so, Israel is called upon to draw other nations into this covenant of blessing with her God.

In reading the Hebrew Scriptures, we learn that Israel never fulfills her call. She still awaits the coming of the Messiah and cannot overcome her own brokenness. This covenant blessing, however, is fulfilled in Jesus Christ who draws other nations and peoples not to the land but to the foot of his cross. His sacrifice and blessing on the cross offers us not a plot of dirt but a restored relationship with his father. This good news is shared not by the twelve tribes of Israel, but through twelve disciples who carry the message of redemption to the four corners of the world. They share the gospel message with all who feel guilt, shame, and condemnation.

The Good News is preached and taught that the bond between God and us is restored. Consequently, we can take our place as adopted sons and daughters of God. In doing so, we become inheritors of his kingdom. This inheritance is not a future hope; it is a present reality! Through the work of Christ on the cross, we move from the weeds to the wheat.

This journey into the kingdom is a conscious choice we make daily through the way we think, act, and feel. Every moment of every day, we have a choice to make as to how we are to live our lives and how we respond to what people and fate put in our path. Our choices, however, should be informed and directed by the "still, small voice of God" who speaks his blessings to those who take the time to pray, meditate, read, and study the Scriptures.

Listening for the voice of God requires that we cultivate a humble spirit, opening our spirit to be moved in surprising directions. This sacred movement of discovery also requires patience and learning how to read God's timing. By doing this, we move from being controlled by our time to moving into divine time—that perfect moment when all things come together.

When we operate in God's time, the obstacles are removed. The way is now open to enter into his will. These simple core values open us to see the blessings as we respond to God in thanksgiving. We discover that our creator is working his purpose out—and that none of our life's experiences are wasted.

Each experience has a mystery that needs to be unwrapped in the maze we call life. When we get there, we can lift up our voices in triumphant praise. Even more than that, we recognize that our God knows us by name and that we are loved. His love becomes so bountiful it cannot be contained within our hearts like Old Faithful in Yellowstone Park, which erupts when the pressure below builds up and finally explodes. The heart explodes and overflows with a love that must be shared. God demands it; it is part of his divine plan for us to enter into a personal relationship through his Son who is an incarnate symbol of divine love.

This movement of spirit is a wonderful journey and gives us the power to let go of things that claim our lives and often appear as illusions of happiness and redemption. In response, our heart abounds with thankfulness. When we are overwhelmed with thanksgiving, we are compelled to share our gift with others.

Chapter Four

CAUGHT IN THE WEEDS

ROCKY stopped by my office as he normally did when he was in the area. As he sat down across from me, I knew this visit was not going to be a social call. Although he is a few years younger than I, the wrinkles on his forehead and around his eyes revealed a lifetime of worry and anxiety. Each line on his face, I suspect, can be traced back to a raw emotion that gripped his life and caused many a sleepless night. Each wrinkle represents a poor decision he has made in his life. The crisis may have passed years ago; the evidence of the events, however, is still evident.

Many of us think that we can easily hide our deepest emotions, but our faces reveal the truth. No matter who we are or where we live in the world, our expressions and our emotions are universal; they speak loudly to those who have learned to read body language. Words can reveal a lie, but our faces usually speak the truth. Consequently, I could see that Rocky's face spoke volumes.

Rocky is in his early fifties. He is not somebody who just walked off the streets; we have been friends for years. A salesperson by vocation, he comes into my office in his working attire, white shirt, tie, and neatly pressed slacks. Over the years, he has sold just about everything; like most good salespersons, he is one of those people who can sell you anything. For a good salesperson to succeed, all it takes is the gift of gab and developing a trusting relationship with his or her clients. Moreover, good salesmen are not selling a product—they are selling themselves. By combining these factors, such people make a lucrative living. In his time, Rocky had made some good money, but he has had some downturns as well. This was one of his bad years. Consequently, I intuitively know that this is going to be a serious visit.

When people take the time to come to my office, it is for good reason. They sit in my office in joyful moments to share the good news that they are getting married and would like to have the service take place before God and in his church. They come to my office because they have just celebrated the birth of a child and they are seeking the sacrament of Baptism.

In such moments, they are acknowledging the gift that was given them; they are seeking to bring a child into a covenant relationship with God. People and couples come to me when they arrive in town to look for a spiritual home. Practically speaking, they have discovered that the church is one way to find instant community.

There are those who sit across from me because they are hurting, having lost someone who is dear to them. In their grief, they are seeking to work through their loss, and they are seeking to find closure in their lives. Rarely does someone pop in my office to pass a little time and just visit. Either they are too busy or too consumed by their time restraints to just come in and say hello.

The bottom line I have learned over the years is that when people come to my office, more often than not, they are looking for answers, especially if they are in a crisis. My job is to sit and listen as they reflect on what is taking place and causing their trauma. I am there, not to give them the answers, but to help them find the answers that are found deep within their souls.

Too often in moments of crisis, we seek to find answers outside of ourselves rather than looking within. As Rocky settled into his chair, he got right to the point. He wanted to know if he had been cursed! At first, I was startled by his question. I quickly mentioned that I had never had anyone come in with such a question. He went on to explain that nothing had been going right in his business for months. The more he tried to generate sales, the more he failed; when you live on commission, the result can quickly become an economic disaster!

He was in trouble. He went on to say that every business deal he put together seemed to fall apart and evaporate just when he seemed so close to consummating the deal. All he had to do was complete the final paperwork, gather a few signatures, and collect his commission. Rocky lived off his commissions; with the loss of each transaction, he found himself going deeper into debt. Sadly, he had already filed for one bankruptcy, and he was on the edge once again. His credit had dried up and, since he had previously tapped his family and friends for financial assistance, the well was dry. With everything going wrong, Rocky had concluded that someone had cursed him with an evil spell or hex. More importantly, he was desperately seeking ways by which he could break this spell.

In his story of financial woe, Rocky symbolizes all of humanity who believes that when something bad befalls them, or when they are the victims of recurring personal problems, then they must be living under a curse. Paradoxically, there is some truth to this statement, which forces us to raise a question: Who or what can bring about a curse?

Turning to the Scriptures for an answer, we can open up the book of Genesis and immediately read about the curse that was brought on by Adam's disobedience to God. After Adam and Eve ate from the tree in the garden and deliberately disobeyed God, God pronounced his judgment. God cursed the serpent who had tempted Eve. Then God cursed the ground that they walked on. In addition, Adam would have to toil for his food, and Eve would have painful childbirth. Moreover, both Adam and Eve were banished from paradise (Gen. 3).

If we read this passage literally, we also have not escaped the declaration of this curse. Throughout human history, humankind has had to toil in the ground to survive. Life has been hard. Nevertheless, do we dare to read the Scriptures from a literal perspective? The ancient Hebrews fully understood that their scriptures were based on an oral tradition that was passed down from generation to generation. This passing on of the sacred stories to countless generations went on until someone had the time, education, and ability to write down these orally transmitted events.

Consequently, these Hebrews would not read the Pentateuch, the first five books of the Hebrew Bible, from a literal prospective. They understood that if God's truth was going to be revealed, they had to search a passage and find its truth deep below the surface of the written word. Each word and each letter of the word had significant meaning, which meant that each story and each word would add to the interpretation. As a result, it has long been accepted in the academic world, both in the Hebrew and Christian traditions, that the Bible was written by the hand of mankind, but it was inspired by God.

God was telling his story through human experience, but this story has many layers. Each layer needs further interpretation, prayer, and study. Equally important, as we peel back the layers of the stories, we must call upon the work of God's Spirit to guide us in our search for truth. For these reasons, we can explore a story and think that is says one thing—only to discover a deeper truth at another time!

Only through the process of discovery can we be touched by the Spirit of Truth. We must be open and willing to move beyond the literal word and enter the world of paradox. In our search, it is in paradox that we encounter the wonderful mystery of God. God speaks to us through the gift of language. Jesus was well aware of this principle; he often cloaked his stories in mystery and paradox. For example, Jesus taught that whoever wants to save his life must lose it and whoever loses his life for His sake will find it (Matt. 10:39).

In Mark's gospel 9:35, he says whoever wants to be first must be last. These are incredible statements, and I have no doubt that as Jesus made these proclamations, his audience had puzzled looks on their faces. These mysteries, however, would not be fully realized until the resurrection of the Christ. In his resurrection appearances, we read that he spent a great deal of time teaching and interpreting the Law of Moses, the Prophets, and the Psalms. Jesus opened their minds to the meaning of his puzzling statements in Luke 24:46–47.

Let us take a journey and look at the first three chapters of Genesis and the curse of Adam. In the beginning of creation, God speaks through his Word and Spirit; as a result, the creation is formed. Through the spoken word, he calls into existence the light, which he calls "good." He then calls for the expanse of the sky and the separation of water from the land. Upon the land, he creates vegetation, plants, and trees for the bearing of fruit. The creation now has a sense of order, purpose, and abundance. He continues his creative process with the creation of animals great and small. In addition, he brings forth fish and other living creatures to fill the oceans. Then, gazing upon his wonderful and glorious creation, he blesses the fruit of his creative word and calls it good! As the scene is set, he calls into creation His most precious gift, humankind.

When we move into Chapter 2, we discover the second creation story of humankind, that of Adam and Eve. Next, a dark chapter rolls in like a powerful, violent thunderstorm. In the peacefulness of the garden, after God had instructed Adam and Eve that they were not to partake of the fruit of the tree of knowledge, the stage is set for the great fall. Evil, in the form of a snake, quietly slithers into the lives of these two people. Eve is tempted by the words of the crafty snake to eat of this very fruit.

We immediately discover that words can be used for good or evil. Innocently, she submits to his temptation.

Seeing no consequences for her actions, she shares the fruit of her experience with her mate. Adam accepts the argument that the fruit is good, pleasing to the eyes and rich with wisdom. As the ancients tell the story, there is no turning back. A decision is made after little or no discussion. They make their choice! Their eyes are opened, and they can see their choice is bad. Adam and Eve have disobeyed God, their eyes have been opened, and they will have to face the consequences of their actions. As a result, we are left with a legacy of being children of the curse! The concept of being "cursed" is introduced to the drama of human experience and waits to spread its damage for generations to come.

The word "curse" resonates with powerful sound when it rolls off someone's lips. It creates a negative field that engulfs everyone and everything in its grasp. Just the mention of this word can cause shivers down one's spine. So, when God speaks to the serpent in Chapter 3:14, it should capture our full attention.

> Cursed are you above all the livestock and all wild animals! You will crawl on your belly and you will eat dust all the days of your life. And I will put enmity

between you and the woman, between
your offspring and hers; he will crush
your head and you will strike his heel.

Before we venture any further, we must ask a
question. Did God truly curse the snake—or is it just
a metaphor? In the scheme of nature, snakes play a
vital role in the balance of nature itself. How can they
be a force of evil? Consequently, we discover that God
is conveying his story through the use of symbols,
hyperbolae, and metaphor.

This word "curse" as defined in our English
dictionaries as the calling of supernatural powers to
send injury upon or the calling for the damnation
of a person or object. It stands in direct opposition
to that which is good. The concept of cursing will
grow and take on many different lives as its use moves
from culture to culture. For example, curses are found
throughout the Bible—from the Hebrew Scriptures to
the New Testament. In exploring the Scriptures, we
have to prepare once again to enter into the mystery
of paradox.

In the New Testament, the curse oddly enough
plays a central role in the story of redemption. St. Paul
explains in Galatians 3:13 that Jesus redeems us from

the curse of the law by becoming a curse for us. The law, which is given by God, brings forth blessings and curses. The curses take on shape as early priests and scribes begin to define the law.

St. Paul recognizes this strange contradiction. "Anyone who is hung on a tree is under God's curse" (Deut. 21:23). This statement becomes extremely problematic during Jesus' life and ministry. Everyone in the time of Christ clearly understood that if an individual was hung on a cross, it was because they were living under a curse! St. Paul insightfully sees that the cross, which was once a symbol of a curse, had become a symbol of life and blessing. In other words, Jesus takes on the curse of mankind—death— by allowing himself to be nailed to a cross. It is a sacrificial act of love, mercy, and forgiveness that opens the door of redemption through which we are freed from the curse of Adam.

Moving back to the central point in the story of the fall, who ushers in the curse in this story of human drama? Is it the snake that only made a tempting suggestion? We can easily say yes! It is his fault. He knew what he was doing; through his creative word, he made an offer Adam and Eve couldn't refuse. On the other hand, where is God's culpability? The word "curse" comes from his lips. If God is all-knowing, he should have foreseen the stress he places on the first couple.

When we think about it, God has only pronounced the consequences of the dreadful decision made in the garden. After all, God gives Adam and Eve fair warning. All of paradise is theirs; all they have to do is stay away from the tree of knowledge. This leaves us with the first couple. They consciously partake of the fruit. They make a conscious choice and put their thoughts into action. The actions bring about the consequences of their thinking, feelings, and actions. When they partake of the tree of knowledge, didn't they bring about their own destruction? Did they not bring about their own curse?

Too often when bad things happen, many of us assume we are being cursed and punished by God. People never stop to think that God's ultimate nature is love. If love lies behind his actions, how can he bring harm to his beloved people? God cannot-and will not violate his own nature, it is impossible for him to do so! Out of his love, however, he will not take away our freedom of will. Consequently, God may allow us to suffer the consequences of our actions, but like the story of the first fall, he is there to redeem us from our mistakes and poor choices. Can it be true, therefore, that the dictionary was wrong in trying to define a curse as an action of some deity? And how did such definitions evolve? Let's look at a few examples.

In the ancient Greek and Roman cultures, curses were generated by writing down the words of a curse on a tablet and calling forth some spirit, demon, or deity to bring about suffering or injury to another party. The words they used were like a prayer and had power to accomplish its goal.

In the Celtic world, people believed that curses could be accomplished through the use of eggs! It was a common belief that if you buried an egg on another person's farm, you would destroy the land's fertility and ruin your neighbor's crops. In the Egyptian world, there was a broad-based belief that if you violated the tomb of a Pharaoh, you put your life in danger and became susceptible to the curse of the mummy. Thus, the curse of King Tut was born.

Throughout the ages, people have believed that curses, incantations, and graven images had mystical power and were a living reality—and that places and objects could become a destructive way to control people and events.

These beliefs are so entrenched that they live on in our culture. Just ask any sports fan. For instance, take the Boston Red Sox baseball team. It was long held that a baseball team could be veiled with a curse. For decades, it was believed that the "Curse of the Bambino," Babe Ruth, had long haunted Boston. With this curse, the team would never capture a World Championship. The Red Sox finally won the World Series in 2004. What changed to break this curse? During those difficult years, it was easier to blame the lack of success on a curse instead of looking at the talent, coaching, and management of the team. Such stories help fuel the perception that if someone or something continues to encounter misfortune, there was a good reason—they were cursed by some mystical and evil power. Consequently, the dark shadows of curses reach out their tentacles throughout the world and into every culture and generation. The consequences are obvious; the idea of curses resides deep within the soul of humanity.

Let us turn back to Scripture to explore the origin of the curse. To do so, we need to return to the book of Genesis. When Genesis was written, the ancient Hebrew people were attempting to answer a question that we have all asked: What is the origin of evil? How does it exist? And why do we have to fight to overcome its curse? The astute reader of Genesis will note that the author does not attempt to answer the question regarding the origin of evil, i.e. the serpent. All they know is that evil exist.

The closest we come to an answer to this question is that "evil" is a fallen angel (Luke 10:18). Take note that the serpent just happens to show up in the Garden which is, in itself, problematic. How could something that is crafty, cunning, and evil co-exists with that which is good, holy, and pure? The Garden, as God had created it, was to be heaven on earth. That being the case, why do we find evil in the midst of the good? The answer is quite simple: evil and good co-exist.

We witness this reality every day when we look in the mirror. When we see ourselves, we see a person who has the capacity for both good and harm. All that is needed is the right moment or circumstance to trigger our actions. Just as troubling, we have to accept the reality that evil has always been a part of the human existence; recorded history bears out this fact. So, we struggle to understand the origin of evil and the curses associated with it. We fight to overcome its power in our lives. Yet, despite its influence, or maybe because of it, we discover what it means to be redeemed—and that we need a savior to save us from ourselves. Such acts of salvation are gifts from God and can be found in many places around us.

Recently, I had the wonderful opportunity to attend a sweat lodge ceremony on the Puyallup Indian Reservation in Washington. The lodge, or "inupi" as Native Americans call it, is a sacred place of purification. The lodge is a tent-like structure constructed of large willows woven together to form the main frame. Then the "inupi" is traditionally covered with hides or other material to seal it. With this particular "inupi," tarps and blankets work just as well. The structure, when complete, offers a totally dark environment except for the glow of red-hot, large stones that are placed in the fire pit. The fire pit is found in the middle of the structure. This sacred structure is a place to pray, to meditate, to learn, and to spiritually cleanse oneself. Native Americans have long upheld the sacred nature of this tradition and adhere to a strict protocol for the ceremony, which is led by a spiritual elder.

On this particular day, I was there to deal with my own demons and purify my soul from the curses that secretly hid in the dark recesses of my soul. They had lay hidden from me for many years. Furthermore, I was able to trace them back to my experiences in the Vietnam War. Even though forty-two years had passed, I was still under the curse of the war. It was time to cleanse myself from thoughts and feelings that influenced my choices in life.

There are four parts to this sacred ceremony; each session is called a round. Each round can last thirty to forty-five minutes. Each round addresses various stages of our lives. In the ceremony, you enter the "inupi" and gather around the fire-pit of heated stones, starting with about nine stones. More stones are added after each round—until forty-two stones fill the fire pit.

In each round, you are surrounded by darkness; during each sacred round, the elder guides you with words of wisdom, song, and prayer while offering gifts of sage and tobacco. Throughout the ceremony, the elder sprinkles water over the stones with a cedar branch as he offers up his prayers and the prayers of others. As the water hits the stones, you hear a hissing sound as it immediately evaporates. The steam fills the "inupi" with a fragment aroma.

On this day, the lodge ceremony was designed to meet the spiritual needs of veterans, especially those of us who had experienced combat. Not surprisingly, there were a number of us from the Vietnam War. Each of us was living with our own memories and secrets from the war; with each negative memory, we had to contend with a curse that claimed parts of our lives. There was not one of us who did not carry a secret wound into that "inupi."

We try to bury these wounds from others and ourselves. And like our WWII counterparts, we have learned to hide our secrets from others. I did not know that when you enter a combat zone, there is an unwritten rule that you just do not talk about your experiences. The tragedy is that we knew nothing of post-traumatic stress (P.T.S. or P.T.S.D.) back then. We just knew that we were haunted by our nightmares; we became suspicious and vigilant of those around us; we were easily startled; we were prone to uncontrolled flashbacks. As a result, we tried to heal ourselves through various sorts of dysfunctional behavior. These behaviors are thought to be medicating, but the only thing we did was open the door to drugs and alcohol abuse. Worse yet, for many vets, healthy relationships with wives and children eluded us.

In the ceremony, the elder took us on a different path in the fourth round. He called it "the dark man." As his voice softly pierced the blackness of the "inupi," his words took shape in the animals he called forth. The dark man is the trickster or the joker in our lives. He lives in the world of opposites. His role in life, much like the snake in the Garden of Eden, is to lead us down the wrong path. The dark man is symbolized in the animal kingdom by the blue jay, crow, or coyote.

In this sacred dance of the mind, one has to acknowledge that the joker has his way with us in the choices we make in life. He camouflages his deeds in things that appeared good. We are looking for wheat, but find ourselves in the weeds. As a result, we end up in a place we do not want to be. We learn that evil is just as big a mystery as the concept of God. Many of us do not consciously choose to be open to the dark man or his tricks, yet we fall victim to the joker. I cannot tell you when the joker first started to appear in my life, but now I have a new name and concept to understand its influence. Equally important, I was able to seize the moment to open myself up to cleansing its influence from my life.

When I left the ceremony that evening, I recognized that the joker had had its way with me, but the miracle that took place that day was that I could now laugh at myself and all the mistakes I had made. I could see that the joker taught me a lot about myself and the choices I had made in life. Those experiences were not lost! They became acceptable parts of my life, which I accepted and use to make different choices.

Leaving that "inupi," I confronted the mystery of the joker. At first, it was puzzling. When this miracle of insight took place, I understood that my vision of the past became more and more clear. I knew there was a change in my thoughts and attitude after I emerged into the daylight. This experience was somewhat a mystery, but I did understand that healing had to do with my freedom to choose, my choice to go to the reservation, my choice to do a sweat lodge ceremony, and my choice to rid myself of my nightmares and my past. Choice is always a major component of whether or not we walk amongst the wheat or the weeds. This principle is quite clear when we read the sacred stories from the Scriptures.

Looking back at the Genesis story, we witness this truth. We see how God instructs Adam and Eve— before and after the fall—through his word. His word can and does influence the choices we make in life. In Genesis, God tells Adam, "Don't eat of the fruit of the tree of knowledge." Adam and Eve have a choice to make. Do they follow God's admonition? No. In failing to do so, do they take their lives into their own hands? Do they bring about their own curse?

The answer is glaringly right before us; it is found in knowing the power of freedom of choice.

Freedom to make choices is one of God's most precious gifts. This is one gift that will never be taken away. This precious gift from God is fundamental to understanding the subject of blessings and curses. Is the curse that befalls mankind in the creation story the result of God's actions? God curses the ground and the serpent, and sentences mankind to a life of toil and pain. Is God so capricious that he offers his blessing one moment and a curse the next?

Let us take a closer look at the story. God instructs Adam and Eve not to eat of the fruit in the Garden. Adam and Eve are equally guilty; each of them makes a choice not to follow God's instruction. The curse that results does not come from God. God cannot curse that which is made in his image. To do so, he would be cursing himself.

If we accept the premise that God is all good and all loving and evil does not dwell within his being, how could such a curse come from his lips? Is God so erratic that he blesses his creation one moment and curses it the next? Doesn't God need to be consistent and true to the essence of his being if we are to trust and follow him?

When we search the Scriptures and study his creation, we learn that God is consistent. He never changes his nature. And even more importantly, in God's love, evil and good cannot co-exist and occupy the same space. God cannot curse his creation; it is not within him! The curse that results from the fall of mankind is brought about by the choice Adam and Eve make. And if we follow this logic through the Scriptures, we see how each time someone finds themselves in trouble, it is because of the choices they make in life. Consequently, Adam is not cursed by God; Adam curses himself by failing to be obedient to the law that God uses to govern the kingdom.

So, as Rocky laments over his life, financial setbacks, and lost contracts, he naturally assumes that he is cursed. It never occurs to him that the situation in which he finds himself is caused by his own poor choices. Oftentimes when he has a hot contract pending, he is already spending his commission before the deal is finalized. To make matters worse, when he writes the contract, his client is often on shaky ground, which makes the contract somewhat questionable. When the contracts fall through, Rocky finds himself in deeper financial trouble.

The more I listen to Rocky, the more I recognize that his actions are an ongoing pattern in his life.

Sometime in his early history, he set himself up with this pattern of behavior; worse yet, he never makes the connection between the patterns in his life and his success or failure. He does not recognize that the decisions we make set up the patterns of our lives. And the patterns we develop become habits and have consequences. Then, when all hell breaks loose, we wonder what happened. What went wrong? Why do we feel cursed? Why do we find ourselves standing in the weeds?

Chapter Five

GUIDES

IT was my good fortune to cross paths with an old friend eighteen years ago. When I first met Bill, we immediately became friends—despite the fact he had somewhat of a colorful past. I was told that had we met in his younger years, our friendship would not have developed. Back then, Bill was very active in his alcoholism. He was not just an alcoholic; he was one of those individuals whom booze made mean. Even Bill admitted that he was not a very nice person and often hurt people, especially those closest to him.

If you were to meet Bill today, he is a different person. He had years of hard work behind him in his recovery process, and he worked hard in Alcoholics Anonymous. In his process of recovery, he developed the virtues of patience, gentleness, kindness, faith, love, and peace. Through recovery, he was transformed. Equally as important is that Bill has taken on the role of guide, to lead others who suffered in the same way as he did. In AA, these guides are called sponsors.

A sponsor is an individual who has successfully enjoyed sobriety for a number of years. Their success is due in part to being active in meetings and discovering all the land mines that lie below the surface of souls that can easily explode if they are not careful. Even more importantly, guides have learned the secrets of living in healthy, loving relationships. Having successfully learned to live out a recovery program, these individuals become sponsors and work with new members to walk them through what is called the "Big Book," the AA manual for recovery.

Sponsors meet regularly with their charges to talk and be a sounding board as they struggle in their efforts to remain sober. Because of their own history, sponsors have the experience to see when someone is living in denial and to offer wisdom to help these souls make right decisions. As one of these sponsors, Bill has long been a guiding light to those who live in the darkness of their addiction.

Bill's role in the AA community reinforces for me the importance of relying on guides when we find ourselves in uncharted waters—not just in the recovery process, but also in other areas of our lives. When we look around our social environment, we encounter a plethora of people who become models in our lives, though we may not call them sponsors. We know them by other titles, such as mentors, leads, coaches, counselors, teachers, or spiritual directors. No matter what title they are known by, they all have the same role: to guide people in their daily lives and chosen professions.

Guides have always been essential to the growth and development of every culture or group dating back to when we still lived in caves. Guides are part of the fabric of achievement. Moreover, they are a critical component to those who are lost. These lost souls have somehow lost their ability to think rationally, act responsibly, feel normally, and love successfully. Somewhere along their journey, they have become confused, filled with doubt, and unable to see the consequences of their decisions.

Experiencing one of the dark episodes of my life, I discovered that when you are hurting, you cannot see the future because you are too busy trying to medicate the pain or loss in the present. In such times, it is even difficult to recognize that you are standing in a field of weeds that are ready to consume you. Therefore, you continue to act out, oftentimes with deleterious results to those who love you. Equally as tragic, these lost souls continue to repeat the same mistakes—often to the chagrin of others who cannot rationally understand why you repeat your mistakes. These lost souls do not understand that if nothing changes in their lives, nothing changes! They hope for miracles, thinking that the same behavior will somehow produce different results. They cannot harvest wheat when they are only cultivating weeds.

What does it take to make a radical change in your life? The opportunity arises when someone reaches the crisis point and is willing to reach out to another person. The crisis helps to break through our denial and to admit that we cannot rely on our own skills. We cannot be our own savior; we need a guide!

Turning back to the Hebrew and Christian Scriptures, we find that one of the major topics that is woven into the fabric of sacred stories is the subject of guides and guidance. Throughout the many stories in the Bible, we encounter biblical heroes who become guides for God's people. The illustrious list includes such heroes as Abraham, Moses, Aaron, King David, Ruth, and Isaiah. All take on the role of guide to direct God's people to his Word and Promised Land.

In these sacred stories, you often encounter the Hebrew word, "Hodos," which means "guide." In fact, you will witness the word Hodos or one of its derivatives used more than 880 times in the Old Testament. Scholars often say that when you read a passage and a certain word is used over and over again, you need to pay strict attention to what the writer is conveying because the writer is revealing an important concept that they seek to pass on to their audience.

If we explore the word "guide" more deeply, we discover that in the ancient Greek culture, the word denotes an action of walking or taking a journey by land or sea with a particular goal in mind. On such journeys, the Hebrews and Greeks understood that there were always two ways to go. Humankind always had a decision as to what direction they chose. Such decisions were voiced with a word of caution because it was believed that sojourners could go down either the virtuous path or the path of destruction.

What path did people take? It was taught that the path on the right led to virtue, land, or righteousness. The path on the left was a road to nowhere but trouble. As time passed, the word "guide" evolved and took on a more significantly religious meaning. The *Dictionary of Theological Thought* calls our attention to the fact that one was not only guided to make right decisions, but true guidance led to God. This concept of being directed by God, to God, becomes a major theme of biblical stories, and we see it clearly in the book of Exodus.

In this classic story of redemption, God hears the cries of his people as they are held in captivity in Egypt. From Mt. Sinai, Moses is called into service to be an agent of change. Moses is sent back into Egypt to rescue his people and guide them from the land of slavery to the land of freedom "flowing with milk and honey." This land is to be the new Garden of Eden—heaven on earth.

As Moses directs his people on this journey of faith and discovery, he leads them into the wilderness, which becomes a time of trial. The strange twist in the story, if we read it carefully, is that it is really God who is guiding his people. As God guides them using a pillar of fire, God is testing them. He holds out a promise that looks like a blessing, but the Hebrew people view their circumstance as a curse. They voice their discontent, saying that they were better off in Egypt. God, however, is not done with them. Using Moses, God guides them to the water of Miraba when they are thirsty. When hungry, he rains down manna from heaven. When the people complain that they are tired of bread, God provides quails. He provides for all their needs. In return, all he asks is that they walk in his ways and remain in relationship with him (1 Kings 2:3; 8:58). Like all journeys, there is a goal, salvation!

The theme of finding the right way is picked up in the New Testament, especially in the gospel stories. In the New Testament, Jesus is looked upon as a new Moses. As Moses guides his people from slavery to freedom—from Egypt to the Promised Land—Jesus takes them from the slavery of sin to forgiveness and from the Promised Land to the gates of the kingdom of God.

On this journey, Jesus literally "becomes" the way. Unlike guides who went before him, Jesus does not point us to the way; he personifies the way in how he thinks, acts, and feels. Furthermore, when someone literally directs you, there is no chance you can get lost.

I thought about this concept the other day when I had to visit a large Home Depot store. When I got in the doors, I was greeted by a friendly salesperson who inquired if I needed help. I told him that I was looking for a plumbing part. So, rather than directing me to the aisle it was on, he surprised me and said, "Follow me."

I walked a few steps behind him; we weaved our way back through a matrix of aisles until we got to the plumbing supplies. Even then, I was not abandoned. The clerk helped me find the part that I needed and answered all of my questions. As I walked back to the checkout stand, I thought about how helpful it was to have someone lead the way. The early Church recognized this concept and understood that Jesus was not like any other rabbi, priest, prophet, or king. He is a true guide to those who need to be directed from the weeds to the wheat.

This imagery of Jesus as a guide develops fully in the gospel of John. This gospel account is unique because it is the only gospel that records seven "I am" statements. These statements are self-disclosures coming from the lips of Jesus and defining who he is. It is important to take note of the number seven because it is a special number in Jewish theology. The number represents completeness and comes from the thought that it took God seven days to complete creation. Jesus picks up this imagery as he discloses that he will lead us to wholeness as a guide.

This journey to wholeness of the human spirit begins in the sixth chapter of John's gospel. After feeding five thousand people, Jesus declares, "I am the bread of life." The image is clear and powerful; it is the first of the "I am" statements. So, as he begins this self-disclosure, he articulates that he is the very substance that nourishes body and soul. Jesus takes a common and universal substance and transforms it into a powerful symbol that speaks to all cultures and people (John 6:35). In doing so, he is saying, if you are hungry, come feed off me. Let my life, give you life! Take my body, so that I can live in you.

Second, after healing a man who was born blind, Jesus declares, "I am the light of the world" (John 8:12). John uses these powerful stories not to disclose miracles (the apostle never calls them miracles). Instead, he uses the word "signs." These miraculous signs point to a reality and truth beyond themselves. Therefore, when the blind man is given sight, the inference is that he not only receives physical sight, his eyes are opened to see another dimension beyond the physical world—a spiritual reality. In this world of the spiritual, we see truth, we discern good from evil, and we can glimpse into the future to see where the road is leading. Every true guide has this gift of sight.

Third, when Jesus says, "I am the good shepherd," he becomes the symbol of protector of his flock (John 10:14). Even more, unlike a hired hand who may flee at any sign of danger, the Christ even gives up his life for his flock. He places himself between us and that which seeks to destroy us.

Going further with this image, in the fourth "I am" statement, Jesus pronounces, "I am the gate" (John 10:7). This illusion may escape us today, but every first-century Jew knew what he was talking about. When shepherds went into the wilderness at night, they would gather the sheep into caves or build a sheep pen for them. The opening of the pen was left unobstructed. The shepherd would literally sleep at the entrance to the pen. He was there to prevent the sheep from wandering off and to protect the flock from predators. What makes this image more incredible is the relationship of the shepherd with his sheep.

Unlike western sheep herders, where a shepherd drives the sheep in the direction they need to go, in Israel, shepherds lead their flocks with their voice. Sheep have learned to listen to the voice of the one who provides for them. We can extrapolate that the shepherd and the sheep enter into a personal relationship.

The fifth "I am" statement has to be one of the most explosive revelations in human history. Try to imagine this scene. Jesus is notified that his friend Lazarus is gravely ill. When he arrives in the small village of Bethany, just a short walk east from Jerusalem, Jesus is greeted with the news that his friend is dead and already buried! Nothing can be done; what has happened cannot be changed or reversed. Yet, Jesus inquires of Martha, the dead man's sister, where they have laid him.

When he arrives at the tomb, he requests that the stone to the tomb be rolled away. His request is greeted by protest—the man has been dead for four days and will stink! Jesus, however, has already declared to Martha, "I am the resurrection and the life." In this statement of self-disclosure, Jesus is speaking in the present tense. Consequently, he is emphatically declaring that he is the resurrection *now*. This is not a promise for the future, but a present, living reality.

As a sign that Jesus is who he states he is, when the stone is rolled back, he calls out, "Lazarus, come out!" Imagine the silence as the audience waits with anxious expectation to see what is going to happen. Seconds probably feel like minutes, minutes like hours. Each heart begins to beat faster and faster; everyone's mind frantically debates the premise.

Finally, a shadow appears at the entrance to the tomb. As Lazarus emerges with his grave clothes still wrapped around him, Jesus tells the spectators to unbind his friend. Lazarus is to be freed from everything that holds him captive. Lazarus is not merely resuscitated; the gift he was given was much more profound. He is given eternal life, and the raising of Lazarus is a sign of this promise (John 11:1-45).

The sixth "I am" statement follows up on the story of new life. In the fourteenth chapter of the gospel of John, Jesus is preparing his disciples for his own death. He insists that as he travels down this road, his disciples must have faith and trust in his Father. In doing so, he declares, "I am the way, the truth, and the life" (John 14:6). What these disciples did not understand until after the resurrection of the Christ is that Jesus is not pointing to the way, the truth, and the life. He is saying that He is the true reality of what it means to be fully human and living in the abundance of his Father's grace, will, and love. As St. Paul would recognize, Jesus is the new Adam. As the new Adam, Jesus personifies true humanity.

Finally, in his last "I am" statement, Jesus captures the importance of being connected to our life source. Thus, he says, "I am the true vine" (John 15:1). In this statement of self-disclosure, he is stressing the importance of relationship. The imagery stresses the point that if one seeks the abundant life, the righteous life, and life eternal, then one must be connected to that which gives this life—the power of God, working through his son and the Holy Spirit.

This powerful image came to life for me a number of years ago. After a big, wet Wyoming spring storm, the ground was covered by a blanket of snow about six or seven inches deep. With these wet spring snows, the snow was heavy with moisture and weighed down bushes and trees. As I gazed out the picture window, I could see a large cottonwood tree that was in full leaf. Many of its large branches had begun to droop, and one large limb that had broken off the trunk of the tree was resting on the branches below. As I stared at this limb, I said to myself, "How odd. The branch gives all the appearances of being alive, when in reality, it is already dead. It is separated from that which gives it life, and it does not know it."

As the days passed, I continued to observe this living parable and watched this limb succumb to its death; the leaves finally withered and dried up. Separating ourselves from our life source has its consequences as well: death. But we have not been left helpless; Jesus is our guide. In doing so, he leads us to divine truth and opens the doors to knowledge, wisdom, and discernment and new life in him.

The journey to knowledge and wisdom requires that our guides have attained a certain degree of maturity and spiritual development. In essence, they must be acknowledged as master teachers in the community of faith from which they come. This honorable status is bestowed on guides, not by the number of academic degrees they hold. They are lifted up and affirmed because their knowledge reflects wisdom and discernment. This special knowledge is not acquired per se; it is a gift from God and cultivated by one's relationship with the divine. Therefore, God teaches our guides and through them they reach out to those who have an open spirit and are willing to listen.

This chapter becomes a critical building block for understanding our concept of blessings and curses. Early in the history of Israel, rabbis and priests acknowledge that God has a will and that he makes his will known through either direct or natural revelation. These early theologians understand that God expresses his love as he chastens his people.

As we walk in his will, we experience that love and blessing. This love, which is manifested through his grace, will never violate our freedom of will. Yet, when we make poor decisions, we are disciplined. We must always pay the consequences of our own actions.

Nevertheless, divine love is always there to restore us to a state of grace. Moreover, grace lights up the path to peace. In the midst of the weeds, we find our way back to the wheat.

Chapter Six

DISCOVERING GOD'S VOICE

EVERY parent knows that children sometimes make profound observations and speak out with some rather incredible statements. Parents are amazed by their gift of observation and the ability to articulate simply and clearly. Such was the case on a cold, December morning when our oldest son, Tony, entered the kitchen with a piece of paper in his hand and a request on his lips.

At the time, Christmas was quickly approaching. On this particular Saturday morning, I had turned on the television set. A program that caught my attention as I surfed through the channels was a charitable appeal for the people of Biafra.

During the year, northern Africa had been hit with a major drought, leaving the inhabitants with a shortage of water to grow their crops and water their livestock. The results were devastating. Thousands of people were dying, and a national campaign in our country was launched to address the humanitarian crisis. The program was capturing images of young children with extended stomachs, their rib cages showing their bones, and their faces covered with tears and flies. I watched, but I did not see; I listened, but I did not hear. Consequently, when my wife called me upstairs to help her, I easily left the program, not giving a second thought to what I had just witnessed.

When I left the family room, I did not turn off the TV. Tony was only seven at the time, and he continued to watch the program. After about fifteen minutes, he appeared in the kitchen with the paper in his hand. He told me that he was watching a program about starving children, and they were asking for money to feed them. Upon giving me the paper with the phone number, he requested that we take the money we were going to spend on his Christmas presents and donate it to these children.

I was touched to the core of my being. I felt foolish and proud. We had watched the same program, and his heart was touched—and mine was not. We both heard the same message, but he listened—and I did not. Now, as if God was speaking through him, I was being hit right between the eyes! I leaned down to retrieve the number and said, "Tony, I think we have enough money to send to the children of Biafra and still have enough for celebrating our blessings at Christmas." I took the number and quickly called in our pledge. I tucked this story in a special place in my heart to remind me of what Christmas is all about and how it is so important to listen to what comes out of the mouths of children. Children, with their sense of innocence and truth, can often be our guides when we are in doubt or blind to certain life decisions.

In our search for knowledge, wisdom, and discernment, we are often faced with a dilemma about where to look. How do guides help us find our way out of the weeds? How can we discern blessing from curses, especially when they sometimes look the same? In essence, how do we listen to the voice of God?

We have to look back into the history of human development to find a number of written documents that shed light on this question. Each of these documents reveals a glimpse into divine truth; many of these documents contain common threads of comparison. These threads of commonality speak of truth, justice, compassion, mercy, forgiveness, charity, and love.

These documents are the sacred books of many of the world religions. These ancient documents were often shared in part or in whole with other cultures of their time. For example, the Hebrew Scriptures reveal that the early Jews took religious concepts from many of the peoples with whom they had interacted, and then applied those concepts to their own needs to develop their theology.

What made Israel unique was, rather than accepting the premise that there were many gods, the Hebrews understood that there is only one God, Yahweh. Even today, many Christians accept the fact that other religions hold truth—and that God has spoken through their traditions. Nevertheless, Christianity believes that whole truth is revealed in the gospel of Jesus Christ, and this truth is found in the Old and New Testaments.

When we search the Scriptures with their thousands of human interactions with God, we discover a number of ways God has chosen to reveal himself. For instance, Genesis records the creation story, and what we glean from this important story is that the creation reflects the nature of the creator. Just as a painting reflects the thoughts, feelings, interests, and talents of the painter, God speaks volumes about himself by creating nature. We glean his simplicity and complexity while understanding that there is a delicate dance between the two. In nature, we see God's wonderful eye for design, functionality, and beauty. As we stare up into the stars, we greatly admire the mystery and glory of God. With each new sight, we are informed of the nature of God as he silently speaks out through the wonders of that which he created.

When we move deeper into the Old Testament, we also discover that God speaks through visions and dreams. In the fifteenth chapter of Genesis, we find that God speaks to Abram, the patriarch of the nation of Israel, in a vision. Abram is told, despite his doubts, that he will be the father of a great nation. Abram questions God since this old man has no children of his own. Despite all of Abram's reservation, God promises him that he will have an heir. In fact, the patriarch is told to gaze at the stars for his offspring will greatly outnumber them. Through this vision, Abram accepts God's promise and believes that which is revealed. Moreover, Abram is counted as righteous and begins to move on with his life, knowing that God will be there to guide him.

Was Abram special to have such a vision? No! From time to time, each of us is blessed with a vision if we are willing to pay attention. In the last chapter, I shared my vision of the large cottonwood branch. That Sunday, I shared that vision in a sermon using the broken limb as an example of what it means to have the appearance of being alive but in reality being dead. The vision illustrated that death comes when we separate ourselves from our life source. After that worship service, one of the persons in the congregation came up to me and told me that the illustration reflected his life—and he needed some help. Later that week, we got together to begin working out some of the issues that were deeply troubling him.

Indeed, God is true to his word. Abram, through his seed, gives birth to a nation and a destiny. As his legacy lives on, we encounter a powerful story of Joseph and his dreams (Gen. 37). Joseph is one of the twelve sons of Jacob; these twelve sons will each have his own legacy as they form the Twelve Tribes of Israel.

Joseph will have a key role in saving the legacy that was bestowed upon them all. Joseph is given a gift to interpret dreams, especially those dreams that are revealed from God. When we read about Joseph, we encounter how his life is being directed through a series of dreams. These dreams bring both curses and blessings; these dreams bring forth tears of sorrow and tears of joy. Ultimately, we need to look at their source and recognize that dreams are a means by which God speaks through our deepest consciousness to reveal his will and purpose for our lives.

In one of the deepest and darkest times in my life, I was referred to a Jungian analyst who was well trained in dream therapy. Over the months that I was in counseling, I often recorded and shared my dreams with my therapist. Those dreams emanated from the deepest part of my soul, and each dream revealed issues that were screaming to be acknowledged and addressed.

Slowly, as we examined each dream, the dreams became part of a mosaic that revealed a picture of long-suppressed thoughts and emotions. In the end, to my great surprise, I became aware that I was suffering from Post-Traumatic Stress Syndrome. When exploring the root cause to my P.T.S., the trail led me back to my experiences in Viet Nam.

During the mid-sixties, I did a tour of duty with the air force as a security policeman. I worked with a sentry dog in a place called Pleiku. Pleiku was located in the central highlands and had the reputation of being a sanctuary of the VC. Our job in the K-9 unit was to protect the outer perimeter of the airbase at night and secure the base from any enemy infiltrators and sapper teams. The work was scary as we searched the night alone hoping to engage the enemy before they could destroy the aircraft, fuel, or bomb dump. Not only did we have to be concerned about the Vietcong, in the cover of darkness, we were not the only ones hunting. We had to be on guard for a plethora of poisonous snakes and large cats that were also patrolling the night.

To make matters worse, when my dog alerted, I was never sure what type of scent he had picked up or what movement he had detected. Was it a cobra, an ocelot, or an enemy sapper team? There were times that we found ourselves in harm's way as we crept through the darkness.

Early one night, as I was walking out to my patrol area with my dog, I encountered a VC probe. I was caught off guard because Wolf did not alert, and I was not expecting such an early encounter. Nevertheless, I challenged this shadowy figure who was about ten yards from my position. My heart began to beat so hard I thought it would burst. The individual began to move, and I reacted automatically to his movement.

Without thinking about what was happening, I pulled out my .38 revolver and popped off five rounds in rapid succession. After the first round, I was blinded by the muzzle flash of my pistol and could not see a thing. I was not sure if this individual was coming toward me or running away. Soon thereafter, the whole sky was lit up by a flare that was popped by the next guard down from me, but the intruder was not to be found.

After searching the area and settling down, I went to a bunker close to my position, lit a cigarette, and pondered my moment of terror. I realized I was capable of taking a human life! I had just tried to kill another human being. This was not television or a play field where kids gathered to play army; this was the real thing!

While I accepted the reality that I was capable of killing that night, this thought would submerge into my subconscious, only to resurface years later. As a result, when I left Viet Nam, I thought I was leaving my memories behind as I was reentering the world. Little did I know that those frightening memories and encounters would haunt me for forty-five years. Those thoughts found their way into my nightmares.

These negative thoughts forced me to be in constant vigilance, always suspicious when a stranger entered my presence. From time to time, I had flashbacks triggered by a smell, a rainy downpour, or just walking my pet dog at night. Those memories affected many of my thoughts, feelings, and actions. I lost my innocence and trust in people. Moreover, those memories continued to sabotage many of my relationships. As a result, I was standing in the weeds, and I did not even know it! Nevertheless, thanks to a good guide, I found my way. In the midst of my curse, I discovered God's blessing.

Returning to the story of Joseph in the book of Genesis, we come across another important concept that helps us when we are in need of God's guidance and understanding his will. Joseph's story teaches us that God speaks to us through the circumstances of our lives. As each of us lives out our lives, we find ourselves in various situations that at times seem hurtful or destructive.

When Joseph's story is told, we see this process quite clearly. In chapter 37:18, a plot is born out of jealously. Joseph's brothers are resentful of their youngest sibling because he is given the gift of dream interpretation, and he has won their father's favor. Consequently, a conspiracy is woven by his jealous brothers, and the plot is sealed to kill Joseph. Joseph is thrown into a waterless pit in the middle of nowhere. At this point, the unthinkable happens; a caravan of Ishmaelites on their way to Egypt is spotted. After a quick discussion, the brothers agree to sell their bother into slavery, thus taking care of their problem without bloodshed.

The caravan comes at the right time and in the right place to unknowingly enter God's plan. Furthermore, circumstance continues to play a major role in this story of redemption. Upon reaching Egypt, Joseph is sold into the household of an Egyptian officer, and the household is blessed. Then circumstance makes its mysterious appearance. Joseph is viciously accused of trying to seduce the wife of his master and is thrown in prison. There, Joseph receives the good favor of the chief guard.

While this drama is unfolding in the prison, the king of Egypt has begun to experience a series of troubling dreams. Worse yet, none of his spiritual advisors can interpret the dreams. Joseph continues to develop his reputation as an interpreter of these night visions while he is in prison.

Eventually, after a number of twists and turns in the plot, Pharaoh learns of Joseph's gift and summons him to the palace. Joseph is able to interpret the Pharaoh's dreams. He advises the king that there are going to be seven years of plentiful harvests; immediately afterward, there will be seven years of drought. In appreciation for this vision, Joseph is rewarded and given a position of authority to prepare the nation of Egypt for this historical calamity.

Amazingly, during these seven years of famine, Joseph's brothers journey to Egypt to look for famine relief. While there, they unknowingly encounter their brother. When the brothers learn who Joseph really is, they are frightened to death. They think that Joseph will seek revenge! However, Joseph speaks to their fears as the tension builds in this confrontation. He tells his siblings that their initial crime was meant for evil; God, however, intended it for good! Joseph's understanding of the situation paves the way for his brothers and the rest of the house of Israel to stay in Egypt. The story of redemption stays alive as God works slowly and quietly in the circumstances of a guide named Joseph and his people whom we know as the nation of Israel.

A good guide will always challenge us to look at the rhythm of our lives and peer below the surface of unfolding history. Things happen for a reason, and guides will help us to look at our circumstance to see how God is working his purpose out. Many times, this purpose is unclear; oftentimes, we cannot see it ourselves. We need someone with spiritual maturity and wisdom to help us see what is unfolding before us. The circumstances in which we find ourselves can be difficult or troubling, but those same circumstances may be the means by which God is speaking to our souls.

The circumstances in our lives are related to the gift of time—not ordinary time, but God's perfect time. When I was young, I never understood the significance of timing in my life. As I sought to remain in control of my unfolding history, I tried to make my own time. I pushed the limits of what I wanted to do and when I wanted it done. The Scriptures, however, helped me come to terms with the revelation that God often acts at the right moment.

A primary example of this concept is found in the birth of Jesus the Christ. Why was Jesus born in the first century? St. Paul explains that Jesus comes at the right time (2 Cor. 6:2). What is this right time? History reveals that Roman rule is well established throughout the Western world. With Rome acting as chief architect to the civilized world, her armies bring order and peace as she reaches out and conquers one nation after the other with her strength. To move and supply these armies, Rome has to build and secure roads throughout her vast domain.

Commerce is vital to a growing and thriving civilization, which means that Rome has to open and secure new trade routes. However, commerce is not the only thing that is moving along these caravan trails; these roads are an information highway that is used to communicate new ideas, trends, philosophies, and religious thoughts.

People today fail to realize that Rome brings a certain peace to the world after she expands her interest. True, Rome rules with an iron fist, but as long as people obey her laws and pay their taxes, they are left at peace and given opportunities to conduct their business, practice their customs, and explore their cultural and religious beliefs. The roads that Rome builds for her own means are the very roads that are used to spread the gospel of Jesus Christ throughout the world! Being a good guide, St. Paul understands what is taking place in history; without hesitation, he introduces us to the concept of God's time—that perfect time when he will act in history and within our lives.

Luke 1:26 tells the story of the annunciation. In this incredible story, an angel visits a young girl in Nazareth. As the drama unfolds, we learn that this young maiden is from the house of David, and she is a virgin. This is not the first time a celestial being is recorded as making an appearance in the drama of humanity.

In the Hebrew Scriptures, we find a number of events when angels have fulfilled various roles in their service to the creator. In Luke 1, we find the angel Gabriel fulfilling the role of messenger. In fact, when we look at the root word "angel," we discover that the word means "messenger." Although the appearance of angels is limited for most of us, we all have encountered times in our lives when someone provides a comforting word or unlocks the solution to a disturbing problem. In our appreciation for their counsel, we often refer to them as "angels." Whether they appear in a spiritual form or a physical one, they still fulfill the purpose for which they are sent into our lives—to provide a word of wisdom, warning, discernment, or knowledge. From the beginning of recorded biblical history, angels have been one of the means by which God reveals his purpose and will.

In the case of our young maiden, Mary is merely a child—probably no more than thirteen or fourteen. She is betrothed to an older man named Joseph. The message that she is given has all the potential of being a curse. Because she is engaged to Joseph, the act of conceiving a child makes her an adulterer and subject to Jewish law. Adultery is a crime punishable by stoning.

In God's hands, however, this curse is transformed into the greatest blessing of all time. Mary is informed that she is to give birth to a child. The conception is a mystery that has baffled humankind for centuries, but we are informed that it will take place through the power of the Holy Spirit. What will become clear in time is that the child who is to be named Jesus will be the son of God, and Jesus will usher in the kingdom of God. Mary is somewhat dubious about this call upon her life, but despite the inherent danger, she accepts the messenger, the message, and the role that God has given her.

God, however, is not done with her. When we hear God's voice and seek his purpose for our lives, we can test the Spirit as we seek affirmation. At the end of Gabriel's visit with Mary, Mary is told that her cousin Elizabeth is also with child. What makes this announcement somewhat strange is that Elizabeth is an older woman who is past her childbearing years. This child will grow up to be John the Baptist. This is affirmation for Mary that nothing is impossible for God. Throughout the sacred stories of the Bible, we always find that when God calls upon our lives, we are also given words of affirmation. In fact, it always behooves us to test the Spirit (1 John 4:1).

Finally, we come to the last concept by which God speaks to us and for those who provide his counsel. This concept is often referred to as "that still small voice" in many Christian circles. This concept is recognized through both the Scriptures and personal experience. Yet, it is still surprising as to the number of Christians who do not recognize the voice of God. The voice comes from the interior of self rather than an external, audible sound like the voice of James Earl Jones.

People often miss God's voice because they confuse this voice for their own. What distinguishes God's voice from ours, however, is not the sound but the instruction. When we hear this still small voice within, we are finding that we are being advised to think, act, or say something that we would not have chosen for ourselves. This voice often causes us to pause and ask, "Where is this thought coming from?" The directive or thought is challenging us to move beyond our comfort zones.

The marvelous example of this concept is found in 1 Kings and the story of the prophet Elijah. In this story, Elijah has just slain the false prophets of Baal on

Mount Carmel. As a result, Jezebel seeks revenge and vows to destroy Elijah. In his weakness, Elijah flees for his life to a mountain sanctuary on Mt. Horeb, the mountain of God. There in a cave, the prophet desperately seeks the voice of God. He looks and sees the wind, feels the earthquake, and experiences the fire, but God cannot be heard.

Then comes a time of silence; in this quiet, sacred moment, Elijah hears the voice of God. God is instructing the prophet to return to that which he fears. Elijah must set out from his comfort zone, do that which is contrary to his psyche, and re-engage the people and his enemies (1 Kings 18-19).

Over the years, as a seeker and guide, I have learned how critical it is to be on constant alert for that still, small voice. When I do, my attentiveness opens the door to many blessings for myself or others. When I ignore that voice, I find myself living under the shadows of a curse. We must continue to remind ourselves that God has a will and purpose for us, and he will make that purpose known through his voice.

God has spoken through his word in Scripture, but the Scriptures teach us that he continues to speak through his creation and special situations called theophany. Through our own experience, we learn that the Almighty reaches out through our dreams and gives us visions of what can be. If we pay attention to the rhythm of our lives, we see God active in circumstance as he gently makes his purpose known. In his wisdom, he has confirmed his will and character through other religions.

In special and mysterious fashion, he sends his angels as messengers of revelation. Moreover, when we take quiet time throughout the day, we can hear his gentle voice resonating deep with our souls. Whatever the means by which the Lord sends word, he will always give us affirmation if we find ourselves in doubt and standing in the weeds.

Chapter Seven

God's Promises of Blessings

IN reading the last chapter, you will have gleaned that the foundation of blessing is based on the words that are found in the Scriptures. The Bible contains thousands of years of recorded human history.

Through the eyes of the ancients, we view the interaction between God and his people and man's interaction with other men. Thus, we gain insight into man's search for meaning—both in search of self and of God. Through all this interaction between God and humanity, we recognize that our creator has a will and purpose for his creation. In addition, we glean that he has made his will known through a number of different mediums.

His purpose is to guide and direct each one of us, individually and corporately. This outreach to the human family is guided by the Holy Spirit, which is manifested through divine revelation. These revelations are first shared through oral tradition, which later become recorded history. Consequently, we have dual authorship: the Scriptures were inspired by the Spirit and penned by human hand. Although we accept these sacred stories as truth, we interpret them by understanding the audience to whom these pronouncements are made. We view them through their historical setting and the language that was used at the time.

Equally important, we acknowledge how the Holy Spirit continues to use these sacred stories to inform our lives today; the Scriptures are dynamic and not static. God continues to speak to each of us personally and to every generation. Having said this, it behooves those who seek God's truth and wisdom to approach the reading of Scripture with caution.

We need to remain cautious because people have used the Scriptures to their own ends. Every generation has been at fault. Throughout history, the abuse of translation has even swept into the Church to support such things as slavery, war, capital punishment, and the role of gender in a community of faith. These abuses are often the result of reading the Scriptures literally and ignoring the rules of good interpretation. It is interesting to note that since the early Jews understood that their historical text was based on oral tradition, they wisely accepted the fact that one must dig deeply into the stories, peeling back the layers of words and sentences, to uncover the richly hidden meaning. Nevertheless, the Scriptures remain a treasure chest of blessings that reveal the divine truth that speaks to the lives of people from one generation to the next. So, the purpose of this chapter is to highlight God's message of blessing.

> The Lord said to Abram (Abraham), "Leave your country and your people and your father's household and go to the land I will show you. I will make you into a great nation and I will bless you; I will make your name great and you will be a blessing. I will bless those who bless you and whoever curses you I will curse; and all the people on earth will be blessed by you." (Gen. 12:1–3)

In this short revelation, we acknowledge that God's blessing is not restricted to the patriarch of Israel, but is to be inclusive to all nations. This blessing has six movements. First, Abram must leave his father's house and all that is dear to him; this requires Abram to take the first step and move out in faith. Next, God will show him the way. Third, God promises Abram that he will make his name great, never to be lost or forgotten in the annuals of history. So, God's promise will be affirmed. Fourth, God will bless him. In this blessing, God makes his power and presence known in his life. Fifth, the patriarch will also be a blessing to others. This great movement in history will be the direct result of God's will and no other. Finally, blessings will beget blessing; those who bless Abram will also be blessed by God. In this unfolding movement, we extrapolate an important concept: those who curse Abram will bring a curse upon themselves.

In reading the Scriptures, we find that this pronouncement of blessings is found in a number of different passages (Gen. 1:22, 28; 22:15–18). These passages are not just idle words, but history bears witness that this nomadic tribe—with no land to claim as its own—rises to become one of the most powerful forces of its time. Most importantly, God is working his purpose out as he uses Abram's seed to ultimately develop the family line of blessing through which we see the coming of the Christ and the fulfillment of God's word and promise.

A thousand years after Abraham, St. Paul saw this great unfolding of history fulfilled in his own time. With great wisdom and holy insight, the apostle connects the Abrahamic covenant to the universal blessing of all people. "You are all sons of God through Jesus Christ, for all of you who were baptized into Christ have clothed yourselves in Christ. Then you are Abraham's seed and heirs according to the promise" (Gal. 3:26).

Remember that he was writing to a predominately gentile audience. He, therefore, confirms the source and extension of God's blessing to them. But let us take further note: this universal blessing is not without some restriction. We are not blessed so that we are free to do our own thing. Blessings, like freedom and power, come with responsibilities. These responsibilities are best described in "if-then" clauses.

The book of Deuteronomy is a book of the law that is filled with a number of blessings and curses which are based on "if-then" clauses. The blessings are fulfilled only when the people of the covenant adhere to the law.

So if you faithfully obey the commands I am giving you today—to love the Lord your God and to serve him with all your heart and with all your soul—then I will send rain on your land in its season, both autumn and spring rains, so that you may gather in your grain, new wine, and oil. I will provide grass in the field for your cattle and you will eat and be satisfied.

Be careful, or you will be enticed to turn away and worship other gods and bow down to them. Then the Lord's anger will burn against you, and he will shut the heavens so that it will not rain and the ground will yield no produce, and you will soon perish from the good land the Lord is giving you. Fix these words of mine in your hearts and minds; tie them as symbols on your hands and bind them on your foreheads. Teach them to your children, talking about them when you sit at home and when you walk along the road, when you lie down and when you get up. (Deut. 11:13f)

This concept of blessing is quite simple. If you follow the decrees of the Lord, you will inherit the abundance of life. In contrast, failure to act subjects you to a curse of economic disaster and hardship. So, in examining the "if-then" clause, we cannot help but to recognize that whatever happens, the wheels of fate begin to turn with the choices we make.

Think back on your life and focus on the times when you entered into a forest of darkness. How many times did you end up in that dark place because you made a decision and went down the wrong path? Did you violate a moral code or ethical mandate? Did you believe in a lie that you constructed and consequently failed to be honest with yourself or someone else? Did you fail to love God, neighbor, or yourself? Did you become distracted by greed? Did you become confused and forget that the most important priority in your life is to seek the will of God? Did you lose the dream?

If you can say yes to any of these questions, then you have had to suffer the consequences. Amazingly, this profound truth does not have to be revealed by divine revelation; life itself teaches us this lesson. This simple truth seems as if it has been built into our DNA and passed on from one generation to the next.

I suspect that the human family's understanding of the "if-then" clause can be traced back to the Garden of Eden. What we may glean from the Scriptures is that we must learn to recognize the "if-then" clause. When we encounter it and grasp what the Lord's word is providing, our obedience to the precepts will lead us into the presence of the Holy.

Receiving God's blessing is an invitation to enter into his presence. We extrapolate this wisdom by reading a number of passages, especially many of the readings that are found in the Book of Psalms, which awaken us to this reality. King David speaks of the blessing of entering into the presence of God. These blessings are articulated as joy, serenity, and eternal pleasure.

> I have set the Lord always before me, because he is at my right hand, I will not be shaken. Therefore, my heart is glad and my tongue rejoices, my body also will rest secure, because you will not abandon me to the grave, nor will you let your holy one see decay. You have made known the path of life; you will fill me with joy in your presence with eternal pleasures, at your right hand. (Ps. 16)

As we can see, David's jubilance cannot be dampened even in his darkest hours. David's words are profound because we know from reading about his exploits that David was not the most righteous model of human behavior. He lived with blood on his hands and sin in his heart. Throughout his life, like us, he made some poor choices. Nevertheless, David repented, returned to his Lord, and found forgiveness and reconciliation.

> Praise awaits you O God, in Zion; to you your vows will be fulfilled. O you who hear prayer, to you all men come. When we are overwhelmed by sins, you forgive our transgressions. Blessed are those you choose and bring near to live in your courts. We are filled with the good things of your house, of your holy temple. (Ps. 65:1–5)

Everyone who reads and understands the Hebrew Scriptures knows that King David is not a pious saint. Yet, he is regarded in biblical history as one of the great kings of Israel. Even Jesus acknowledges that David is an historical figure to be lifted in praise. Why? I believe what made King David so unique, despite his sinful past, was his constant choice to return to his Lord when he recognizes his transgressions and chooses to step back into the light of God's grace.

David is a character we can look to as we examine our messy lives and the poor choices we make, and say, "We can still have hope and be reconciled." An excellent example of this observation is when we read about David's sinful past (2 Sam. 11–12).

After the prophet Nathan exposes the king's murderous conspiracy and adultery with the woman Bathsheba, we find David offering his act of contrition in Palms 51. In this prayer to be restored to grace, David makes his pleas and implores God not to cast him out of his presence or to take God's Holy Spirit from him.

David desperately needs to have his joy restored to enter into the shadow of salvation. Is it possible? After all, David has the husband of his lover, Bathsheba, ordered into the heat of a battle, ensuring that his odds of survival are greatly diminished. All this is to cover up the fact that David has slept with Uriah's wife and Bathsheba is bearing David's child. This is a plot made for television, but it does not follow the usual Hollywood script.

David is not thrown into prison, and he does not lose his kingdom. He makes a conscious effort to again enter into God's will. We may extrapolate that blessings occur when we choose to enter into God's presence. As we move toward the light, we expose our sins, our rebellion, and our shortcomings. In doing so, our joy is returned, and we enter a state of peace. This spiritual movement leads David to offer a powerful song of praise in Psalm 139.

> O Lord, you have searched me. You know when I sit down and when I rise, you perceive my thoughts from afar. You discern my going out and my lying down; you are familiar with all my ways. Before a word is on my tongue, you know it completely, O Lord. You hem me in— from behind and before; you have laid your hand upon me. Such knowledge is too wonderful for me, too lofty for me to attain. Where can I go from your spirit? Where can I flee from your presence?

David concludes in the rest of his song of joy that there is nowhere to hide from God! To put it simply, David concludes that his only real alternative is to capitulate to the will of his Lord and step out of the weeds and back into the wheat. David tries it his way, but it only leads from one disaster to the next. He tries living in the midst of the weeds and all he experiences is toxicity!

One of the most profound ways we become open to God's blessing is to be aware of teachable moments in our lives. Teachable moments are those special times when God breaks through our denial, stubbornness, blindness, and sin to open our spirit to the abundance of his grace. A teachable moment is an epiphany when the blinders are removed and we see the truth.

> If you love me, you will obey what I command. And I will ask the Father and he will send give you another Counselor to be with you forever—the Spirit of Truth. All (this) I have spoken while still with you. But the counselor, the Holy Spirit whom the Father will send in my name will teach you all things. (John 14:15)

Such epiphanies allow us to change directions, alter our paths, and make different choices that are healthier for our lives and for those people whom we affect in our daily lives. The teachable moments arrive when we allow our closed spirits to open up and become receptacles of grace. A classic example of such a moment is found in Luke's gospel (15:11–31) and the story of the "lost son."

This universal, profound story—which many of us have come to embrace—could have easily been written by us. The story speaks of growing up in a home with sibling rivalries and the lure to leave and explore life on our own. We find ourselves separated from a primary support group and soon discover that we make poor choices that lead us into sin. These sequences of events will ultimately lead to destruction, and all of a sudden we find ourselves sitting in the midst of the weeds. We sit there until we reach a teachable moment when the light of wisdom illumines our darkness.

As the prodigal son journeys deeper and deeper into the weed patch, he reaches the point, spurred on by a crisis, to seek another way. He does so by doing the opposite. Look carefully in his spiraling journey down. In his story, we can see immediately that he desires to be governed by self-will. First, he wants his share of his inheritance now so that he can make his own way in life. Requesting his share of the wealth before his father has passed on is not an outrageous request. In that culture, and in that period, the son could request to receive his inheritance, even when his father is still alive.

What we see in the second step of his downfall is that his self-will is nourished by his selfishness. As soon as he takes these two steps, he has to take the third step to separate himself from those who love him—as if he has totally exposed his soul and needs to hide who he has become.

Fourth, feeling the loss of love and family, he has to feed his emptiness, which opens the doors to self-medication through wild living. Fifth, his spirit has been compromised; his moral and ethical fabric begins to unravel. Sixth, he sees himself for what he has become and his station in life. He loses all that he had! The son is near starvation—physically, emotionally, and spiritually—and is on the edge of his deathbed. The crisis prompts him to open himself and examine where to go from there.

The prodigal son must reverse the thought process that gets him to this place in life. He needs to do the opposite of what he is thinking and feeling. So, by first opening his spirit to enlightenment, this lost son is ready to explore God's Word. Hearing the truth, he takes his second step by developing the resolve to change direction and return to the security of his father's house. From resolve, he physically takes action to reverse his course and turn his life around.

This third action is called "repentance" in the biblical model.

When the lost son repents, he makes the fourth decision: to return home. He needs the assurance of that which is familiar, he needs security once again in his life, and he longs to feel the love of his father and the dream of hope. But notice that when this lost son gets close to home, he is spotted by his father. His father does not wait for the boy to walk up to him. We are perhaps surprised by the father's actions; he cannot conceal his unbridled joy when he runs to welcome his son home.

Immediately, the boy's father restores the status of the misguided young man. He is given a ring, sandals for his feet, and a new cloak, all signifying identity. These loving gestures are acts of restoration; they are the six steps in the reconciliation process. Finally, the grateful father calls for a celebration to honor the flow of grace, which ends the nightmare of self-destruction.

In this seven-step fall from prominence, we also witness a seven-step movement toward blessing. If we look carefully, we begin to recognize the important lessons that each of us must learn along the way. The thoughts and feelings that we embrace—and the actions we take in life—will ultimately create a sequence of events. Each will build on the other to facilitate a curse or promote a blessing! (NIV, Thompson Chain-Reference Bible, p.1617)

This idea should not come as any surprise; just look around and we see this concept everywhere! Watch a gentle storm front move into the mountains. When the rain begins to fall, the rain drops grow larger and turn into a downpour. As the water builds and rushes down the valley walls, it fills a peaceful creek. The creek turns into a torrent as it becomes a ferocious river. Down in the valley floor, everything will be consumed and destroyed as the river becomes an uncontrollable force. There is no escaping this course of events because the sequence had been established; there is no turning back. A curse will always build upon itself; that is the very nature of a curse. The curse is invoked always to bring about destruction. For those who have eyes, this is a teachable moment.

Such teachable moments are found throughout the Scriptures. We see this paradigm in the creation story with the fall of Adam and Eve and how one bad choice leads to the next. In the book of Exodus, we read about the ten plagues of Egypt (beginning at chapter seven and following). The astute reader will take note that the ten plagues were not individual in nature—as if there were no cause and effect of one plague to the next.

With the help of science, it can be argued that the first plague set up the second; the second predisposes the people to the third. The third plague leads to the fourth until that paramount moment when the plagues reach their climax, culminating with the death of the firstborn!

We live in a world of cause and effect. How can the spiritual world escape what we experience in a physical world? Are not the same rules in both worlds in play? Consequently, a curse will build upon itself with its negative energy, just as a blessing will flow out to fulfill its purpose of joy, happiness, and peace. By acknowledging these facts, we don't say that a curse cannot be reversed.

When Jesus was hung on the cross on that first Good Friday, it was said that he was a man cursed under the law (Deut. 21:23). If Jesus were cursed, how could he be the messiah? The answer, of course, is found in the resurrection story on Easter Sunday. The curse of one man became the means of redemption for all men and women. More than that, the blessings of Christ continue to bring on countless blessings for those who seek to live under his rule and grace. But note that we have entered the paradox—we find our redemption through a curse. There is another paradox—out of suffering comes blessings.

> Blessed is the man who God corrects, so do not despise the disciple of the Almighty. For He wounds, but He also binds us; He injures, but His hands also heal. From six calamities he will rescue you; in seven no harm will befall you. (Job 5:17)

The book of Job is one of the most perplexing books in the Old Testament. This book is perplexing because we have to deal with a righteous man called Job who always sought to do the will of God. As a result of his loyalty to God, Job lives a blessed life—until God allows him to be tested by the evil one.

When the story begins to unfold, it soon becomes an enigma. Job's world falls apart; he loses his wealth, family, and all that is meaningful to him. How could this be? Could not God see Job's innocence? Is God not just? Wasn't God powerful enough to stop this tragedy? Why is Job subjected to this suffering?

In searching for an answer, the reader needs to understand that we have four central characters in this drama: God, Job, his friends, and the evil one. Each character is caught up in the tension of the unfolding drama. Job is pulled in two directions; his friends try to make him question his loyalty to God while the evil one tries to destroy him.

In this tug of war of emotions, Job does not grow bitter. He does not lose his faith in God. He does not grow weak. Incredibly, Job's relationship and faith in God actually grows! The events take us right where we need to go—to see the correlation between suffering and blessing. In the end, Job becomes much stronger and more faithful from going through this time of trial.

When we step back from the story, one cannot help but notice that suffering and blessing cannot be separated in the human experience. We cannot experience one without the other. And in this mystical dance of blessings and suffering, we weave a movement that is grounded in faith. In this sacred movement, faith builds character—and character helps us endure the sufferings we encounter in our journey of life.

Look at Job's life; can we see that in the end his blessings are even greater than when he started his journey? He certainly has a greater faith having come through his loss. And in the end, God is no longer a concept that is in his head; God has become a reality that can be experienced in everyday life.

One final note about Job, over the centuries, many people have questioned why God punishes a man who, from all appearances, is a righteous man. To raise the question is to miss the point. God did not cause Job's suffering; it is impossible for God to act in such a way. God cannot contradict his own character, which is love. God, however, does allow the evil one to test his servant in order that Job may grow as a person and in his faith.

Ultimately, by the end of the story, Job receives countless blessings. In the epilogue, some final comments help close the story: "The Lord blessed the latter part of Job's life more than the first. He had fourteen thousand sheep, six hundred camels, a thousand yoke of oxen, a thousand donkeys. And he also had seven sons and three daughters" (42:12f). Job lives on to see his children's children grow up to the fourth generation.

A major theme becomes quite clear to the reader of the Hebrew Scriptures: God will use tragedy to his glory to make his presence known and to assist his people to overcome the hardships of life. In the New Testament, the paradigm of this movement of suffering and blessing surfaces in the life of Jesus and his disciples.

Good Friday has to be the saddest moment in human history. Nevertheless, Good Friday opens the gates to Easter Sunday; both are connected, and you can't experience one without the other. "We also rejoice in our sufferings because we know that suffering produces perseverance; perseverance, character, hope. And hope does not disappoint us, because God has poured out his love into our hearts by Holy Spirit, whom he has given us" (Rom. 5:3f). This hope of which Paul speaks is not unfounded optimism. Hope is the blessed assurance that God is active in our lives—as witnessed by our life stories and the stories of a faith community.

King David acknowledges that God is his fortress and the means by which he is able to seek sanctuary from his enemies (Ps. 144:12). It is through this redemptive process that the people of God will come to know joy and learn the lessons of trust. To put it simply, if God shows that he is on our side, and he is always there for us, so, what is there to fear?

David knew that God was always there to protect him—when he was a young shepherd, when he confronted and killed Goliath, when he fled from

King Saul, when he confronted the enemies of Israel, and when he defended his kingdom from his rebellious son, Absalom. His experiences opened the door to faith. Consequently, no matter what the king had to face, he knew that God would always protect him.

St. Paul picks up this theme as he writes to the churches of the New Testament. Paul, in a number of letters, conveys to the faithful that, through Christ, we have already won the victory—and nothing can plunge us into darkness. For example, in his letter to the church in Colossi, he opens his letter with a thanksgiving prayer.

> Give thanks to the Father, who has guided you to share in the inheritance of the saints in the kingdom of the light. For he has rescued us from the dominion of darkness and brought us into the kingdom of the Son he loves, in whom we have redemption, the forgiveness of sin. (1:12f)

Paul's audience could not help noticing that Paul is speaking in the present tense. Inheritance, rescue, redemption, and forgiveness are present realities! Therefore, he can emphatically state that we have already won the victory. And if we have won the victory, what are we to fear, knowing that God will always be there to protect his beloved?

Imagine what life would look like if every time you encountered a challenge, crisis, or disaster, you felt surrounded and protected by God's grace. Would you still be consumed with anxiety and fear? In all probability, the answer is yes! These emotions are part of the human experience; they are built into our psychological makeup! Fear and anxiety are given to us by God for a reason; they have a role and purpose in our lives.

Nevertheless, when we live in the shadow of God's protection, we experience the fullness of being a redeemed people. We move past the veil of faith into the full reality of a living hope. We are set free! If you have any doubt, Paul succinctly outlines the argument of what it means to live by the Spirit of God (Rom. 8:1-39). He reminds his audience that they have already moved beyond condemnation. The people of God live because Christ lives within them.

The living Spirit of Christ bears witness that we have become children of God. As children of God, we become heirs to the kingdom. Who, then, can deny us this reality? God? Paul says no because God sent his Son to save us. Will Christ, therefore, condemn us? No. He was the one who paid the price for our redemption and continues to intercede for us to his Father!

Paul brings us to the powerful conclusion that nothing can separate us from the love of God that is in Christ Jesus. We are always veiled with the blessing of protection, and God will use all that we experience to his glorious purpose.

Chapter Eight

SOMETHING TO THINK ABOUT

CHRISTIANITY does not have sole possession of truth. Truth can be found in many religions, and these truths often intersect.

God is love. This statement is universally accepted in all three great religions. Many religions share the same thoughts that God is just, merciful, compassionate, and forgiving. In these religious settings, we may argue about the role of Jesus in the drama of redemption and whether or not he is the messiah. The three great religions, however, can support that Jesus manifested the character of God and lived his life in accordance with these values.

One final truth comes from a Chinese parable. Unfortunately, the author is unknown, but he leaves us with something that is germane to the topic of blessings and curses.

There is a Chinese story of a farmer who used an old horse to till his fields. One day the horse escaped into the hills and, when the farmers sympathized with the old man over his bad luck, the farmer replied, "Bad luck? Good Luck? Who knows?"

A week later, the horse returned with a herd of horses from the hills and this time the neighbors congratulated the farmer on his good luck. His reply was, "Good luck? Bad luck? Who knows?"

Then, when the farmer's son was attempting to tame one of the wild horses, he was thrown and broke his leg. The farmers approached the father about his bad luck; his only reaction was, "Bad luck? Good luck? Who knows?"

Some weeks later, the army marched into the village and conscripted every able-bodied youth they found there. When they saw the farmer's son with his broken leg, they let him off. Now was that good or bad luck? Who knows?

Everything that seems on the surface to be evil may be good in disguise. And everything that seems good on the surface may really be evil. We are wise when we leave it to God to decide what is good fortune and what is misfortune. We thank him that all things turn out for good with those who love him.

The ultimate truth of this wisdom story is found in the last line: "All things turn out for good with those who love him." To the Christian, those words may echo the theology of St. Paul. "And we know that God works for the good of those who love him, who have been called according to his purpose" (Rom. 8:28).

This simple belief is the cornerstone of our Christian faith, and we find this truth lived out in the lives of our biblical characters, the lives of the saints, and even in the life of Christ. Think about it! Did Mary think she was blessed when she was informed that she would give birth to the Christ child? How would she explain her situation and save herself from stoning for having committed adultery? Did she think she was blessed having to travel from Nazareth to Bethlehem, carrying this child in her womb in the last month of pregnancy?

After giving birth, did Mary think she was blessed when Joseph told her that they must flee into the wilderness after being informed in a dream that King Herod sought to kill the child? Did Jesus think he was blessed when after his baptism he was forced into the wilderness where he fasted for forty days and was bombarded by Satan's temptations? Did Jesus think he was blessed when he returned to his hometown of Nazareth and the crowd wanted to throw him off a cliff? These were the same people who witnessed his development as a child. These were his former neighbors!

Did Jesus think he was blessed when he realized that the messiah would be betrayed, falsely accused, whipped, and hung on a tree? These are the stories of real life; many of them reflect our own journeys. Mary and Jesus continue on, knowing that all things turn out for good for those who love God, call upon his name, and seek his will. When we find ourselves walking down similar roads and we discover we are in the midst of weeds, our hope and comfort comes from this fact—God is always working his purpose out.

In the opening chapter I introduced you to my daughter. When we learned that Andrina was diagnosed with schizophrenia, I struggled to find the blessings. Fortunately, she did, and her discovery changed her life. She, as a result, had a positive influence in the lives of many people. This is not to say that she did not encounter many hardships along the way. She, however, endured and discovered God's purpose for her. Then came the big surprise for all of us!

Ever since junior high, she had been plagued with an assortment of health conditions. She often fainted, suffered from chronic fatigue, and had various food allergies. It seemed that she was susceptible to every bug that came along. She became an enigma to her doctors because no one could come up with an accurate diagnosis—until an MRI found a tumor in her pituitary gland. Her doctor told her it was too small to worry about, and they would just monitor it.

Her mother and I wanted a second opinion; we flew her out to Seattle to see an endocrinologist. Within fifteen minutes, he knew she was suffering from an auto-immune disease. Sarcoidosis is a rare disease that attacks the immune system. In many cases, after an initial flare up, the disease goes into remission and never surfaces again.

This was not true for Andrina. A year and a half ago, Sarcoidosis almost claimed her life. Her mother and I didn't think she would make it past the summer. She did! After finding a new doctor who was familiar with the disease, he stated that her original diagnosis of schizophrenia was in error. He explained that many of her hallucinations were caused by the Sarcoidosis. The more we learned about this disease, the more we were able to connect the lines to the mysterious symptoms she manifested since junior high. All of her symptoms began to make sense.

Unfortunately, her disease has no cure. Is it bad luck? Or good luck? No one knows. What we do know is that God in his mysterious ways is working his purpose out. We must be patient and trust in his grace. In doing so, we will allow the ebb and flow of life to continue on its way.

If I have learned anything in my twenty-four years of working with people in moments of crisis, I have learned that life always balances itself out. Such crises are like the tumultuous midsummer storms that take place on the plains of Wyoming. These storms roll in out of nowhere; they are violent and beautiful. They crash upon us with gusty winds, sometimes creating tornados. As the thunderheads grow into mountains of clouds and become saturated, they release copious amounts of rain and hail.

Then, as quickly as it comes, the winds and the rains stop, the clouds clear, and we witness a rainbow that mysteriously appears out of nowhere! If you listen carefully, you can also hear mother earth breathing a sigh of relief as she drinks the water that has renewed her life. How often have we taken time to ponder the moment and see the Creator's hand at work, to see his will and purpose, and then relate its lessons to our own lives?

Gail is a person who did just that. Gail is a dear friend whom I met a number of years ago. She had lived through a tumultuous storm that challenged her faith and hope. When Gail's son was twenty-one, he was diagnosed with cancer. Dustin was a bright, young man who was full of life and faith. Unlike most twenty-one-year-olds in the Seattle area, Dustin was a committed Christian who was living out his faith. He was active in a conservative church that catered to the needs of young people. When I first met him, he was receiving inpatient treatment at one of the local hospitals. Despite that fact that he looked perfectly well, his cancer was serious and life-threatening.

As Dustin grew weaker, he and his fiancée decided to get married. The service was performed in the hospital by one of his pastors. Sadly, Dustin succumbed to the cancer and died a few months later. Gail, her husband, and their daughter were devastated! Losing a child is one of the most difficult things a couple must overcome.

The reality is that many marriages are not successful when the loss is too great, the stress too overpowering, and the pain too deep. Many couples find it easier to separate than to continue in a marriage with so many difficulties. Gail and her husband were no exception. Their marriage quickly failed as a result of the death of their son. The loss of Dustin opened the final door of discontent.

Gail and her spouse could no longer hide their grief or hold back the flood of unresolved sadness, anger, and disappointment. For the longest time, these issues were swept under the rug and away from prying eyes. These family issues were never dealt with in healthy ways so they began to manifest themselves in unhealthy behavior. This is not to say that the couple did not try—they even went to counseling—but nothing was going to release them from their past. They had lost the ability to communicate; without communications, they were not able to comfort one another. Dustin's death compromised the marriage even further. Gail and her husband found themselves on the brink of divorce. This thought scared Gail to death.

Gail had married her husband just out of high school. She went from her parents' home right into the home of her spouse. Gail never had a chance to experience what life had to offer. She never explored her own identity because her identity had become woven into her husband and children. Having to live alone was going to offer a whole new set of circumstances for which she was not ready. Within a year, Gail lost her son, got divorced, and had to sell her home. The worst part of this nightmare scenario was that their home contained many fond memories of Dustin. Giving up her home was like giving up her memories of Dustin. Even though Gail still had a daughter whom she loved, Gail still felt the deep sense of loss.

When you experience such a major loss in your life, the care community advises people not to make major life decisions after a traumatic event. If you had experienced a divorce, don't immediately pursue another relationship. If you have lost a loved one, give yourself time to heal and mourn the loss. Don't think that changing your zip code will put your life back together.

Gail did not have the luxury to stay where she was. Her ex-spouse took a transfer out of state and immediately started another relationship. He wanted his share of the equity in their home. Gail was forced to sell.

When the home was sold, Gail called me to share the bittersweet news. The sale of the home became problematic. Where would she go? Gail needed to vacate her home within a month due to a short escrow contract. Gail was not prepared for this moment. She looked at some apartments before she accepted the offer on her home, but she was not ready to live alone. She is an extrovert who needs people around her to draw from their energy. The idea of going to an empty apartment after a day's work was not very appealing—and it wasn't healthy for her. I counseled her not to make a rash decision, but she was in near-panic mode.

After talking to my wife about Gail's dilemma, we concluded that we would offer Gail a spare room that was private and quiet. The room had a lovely view of Puget Sound, a large sitting area, and it was away from the other living areas. It was the perfect place for Gail to have privacy when she needed to be alone and close enough to engage my wife and me when she needed social contact. Most of all, it would offer her a sanctuary where she could take some time and find herself.

At the end of the month, Gail moved her furniture and other things into a storage space and joined our family. We all agreed that this would be a temporary arrangement—I was thinking just a few months. The months, however, continued to roll by, but this did not become an issue. My wife and Gail became the best of friends, and Gail had become an easy person with whom we could share our home. So, there was not any reason to expedite Gail's departure.

As the months rolled by, we witnessed a transformation. Gail became self-assured and was working through her grief. She made great strides and was not the same person who had moved in with us. When she first moved in, she was super sensitive to a male's presence. She was fearful of doing anything that might upset me or cause conflict. It was an interesting experience because she was amazed at how my wife and I interacted. She was still living in her past with many hurtful memories. To make sense of her fate, Gail went into counseling. Gradually, she discovered that she could let go of her old self and discover her true self.

After about a year and a half, Gail was ready to move into her own home. After a number of searches, she found a condominium that she could afford and love. Just as important, Gail knew that she could live by herself and did not need a man to complete her. She had learned this lesson as the three of us shared a number of conversations dealing with marriage and gender roles in marriage.

When Gail finally moved out on her own, she was fully ready. In doing so, she recognized that finding happiness was her own responsibility. Once she found it within herself, love would overflow—and she could share that love. Relationships would be based on how she allowed her love to flow into her beloved—not on trying to make her complete. This is the secret to unconditional love, and this is how God loves us! But, fate was not done with her. Gail needed to take another walk through the weeds.

Shortly after Gail purchased her condo and moved in, a storm was brewing at her place of employment. Each time we saw her, she would give us an update of this ongoing drama. At first, I did not concern myself with the personal issues that go on in most offices. Gail was bright, knew her business, was concerned about her clients, and was conscientious about her job responsibilities. As time went on, however, I began to see her situation growing direr and not resolving itself. Within a few months, she was out of a job. Unemployment was well over 9 percent in our area; a lot of people had given up in finding a job—especially one that paid as well as the one they left.

Upon being released from her company, she collected a small severance package and immediately filed for unemployment. Since her unemployment would only cover a portion of her expenses, she would do odd jobs for friends to make ends meet. In the meantime, Gail began to network with former work associates to get her name out into the business community. One former associate told her that her company was looking for a person with Gail's skills.

If Gail would get her resume to her, she would give it to her manager. The circumstances were just right, and Gail crossed paths with just the right person who might be able to help. In fact, within a week, Gail received a call from one of the managers. After a brief conversation, she was called in for an interview.

Gail had been working with clients from Alaska with her former employer. The new company wanted to break into that market. They needed someone who knew the territory, had all of the right connections, and possessed the experience to set up workshops for potential customers. Gail fit the bill.

Gail's first interview opened the door for a second interview with the department manager. Once again, she made a very favorable impression; within a few days, they offered her the job. When she stopped by our home to share the good news, she was ecstatic! She said, "I found my dream job!"

She would have a corner office on the forty-sixth floor of one of Seattle's tallest buildings. She had a million-dollar view that captured a sweeping view of Puget Sound, the city, and the Space Needle. This would certainly be better than the small, enclosed cubical where she used to work. She would have the option to work from home on occasion. In addition, this new company would subsidize her commute into the city. The only drawback was that she would start at a lower salary, but that didn't matter!

For a year at her former job, she had endured a high stress level due to dysfunctional office politics. She always had to be careful about what she did or said in fear that she would say the wrong thing or have it misinterpreted. All that stuff was behind her.

When we examine Gail's story, did she have good luck or bad? Was she blessed or cursed? Did she find herself in the midst of the weeds only to find the wheat? Who knows? She can only lift up the question to God; only God can decide the outcome.

We are reminded of the need to be thankful for all things and trust that God will always work his purpose out in our lives. This is a simple lesson that is easy to state, but it is hard to live out in our lives. When you lose a child, it is extremely difficult and painful to see God's hand at work. When someone is taken from us, our hearts are filled with sorrow—not thanksgiving.

Our thanksgiving does not arise out of the death of someone, but in our faith in God. God, through Jesus the Christ, has redeemed us from eternal death. And we trust that in his love, mercy, and compassion, he is working his purpose out for the greater good.

In the fog of crisis and trauma, we go to the community of faith in search of answers. We seek out guides who are wise and spiritually mature and who can help us reflect on our lives and circumstances and move us in the right direction.

In a very short period, Gail experienced four traumatic events. The loss of a child, a divorce, moving, and the loss of a job would send many of us off the scales in any stress test. Gail, however, prevailed. These life-changing events did not weaken her; they gave her strength.

Gail's transformation was not an accident. Without really knowing it, she was living out the steps of blessings. First, she needed to learn patience. Patience is a gift from God that becomes learned behavior over time when we see God working in all aspects of our lives. When we learn this virtue, we can believe in trusting in God's time.

As we patiently wait for God's time, this is an opportunity to do some soul work. Our soul work involves letting go of our anger, our hurt, our grief, and those painful disappointments. We work on the negative issues that have shaped our lives and have a voice in our future.

In this time of healing, we must be intentional about seeking the voice of God. To hear Him, Gail had to learn the language of the Spirit. She learned to listen to her inner voice and to test the Spirit that emerged from her soul. She discovered that God can speak even through the circumstances in which we find ourselves. When viewed through the eyes of faith, these circumstances offer those special and rare "aha" moments that connect the past to the present and offer hope for the future.

In the circumstances of life, we can discover the fingerprints of our creator. With discovery of those fingerprints, we can see that God is personally active in our lives. We enter the dance as God speaks through the rhythms of our lives. In listening to this heavenly chorus, God will speak directly to our doubts and questions as he uses the voices of those who surround us.

These messengers from God cross our paths at the right moment in time and say the words that we pray to hear. They play the right chord, and that chord enters the harmony of a beautifully orchestrated measure of time. These messengers make sense of our dilemmas, doubts, and questions. Just as surprisingly, God will take a book that all of a sudden stands out from the other books in our libraries or bookstores—and they speak to our thoughts. The most revealing of these books are the Scriptures. The Scriptures pointed out the reality that Gail needed to pay attention to her dreams. Through the Scriptures, we learn that our dreams unlock the subconscious self and open us to the new channels to hear God's voice.

For Gail to see God working in her life, she needed patience. She needed to understand the concept of God's time. She needed to understand the language of the Spirit. She needed humility. She was humbled by the death of her son, her broken marriage, and her loss of employment. These events shouted loudly in her life that she was not in control!

As much as she wanted to think that she could control her environment, it was only an illusion. Who could blame her? This illusion is a trap into which we all fall victim. The illusion works for us until some event shakes our world and reveals our vulnerability.

A humble spirit awakens us to the reality of our fragile world and opens us to the presence of God. Humility also helps us to gain a teachable spirit.

Chapter Nine

CHOOSE LIFE!

I N the course of a lifetime, who we are and what we have accomplished is determined by the choices we make. Our freedom to choose may be the one thing we can truly control in life. When we are subjected to the cruelty of another person and find ourselves cursed, how we choose to respond may determine the final outcome of our situation. Even when we are subjected to the torrents of nature and victimized by its wrath, we can play the victim or choose to respond in healthy ways. Those who are blessed and those who are cursed have one thing in common: each has the ability to choose how they respond to life.

I recently had a conversation with a friend. Our discussion centered on her relationship with her father. She gave me the rare privilege of looking into her soul. The visions were not pretty. As a child, she was victimized by both verbally and physically by her father. As an adult, she was left with many emotional scars. To medicate her pain, she turned to alcohol to drown those hurtful memories. To her credit and God's grace, she finally realized that she needed to turn her life around; if not for her sake, for the sake of her two children.

She made the decision to give up the booze and live a different life. During her recovery period, she prayed and meditated on her life's story. She entered into counseling and began to take apart those memories that controlled her. It was a tearful recovery, but she finally let go of the painful vignettes that controlled many of her poor choices.

To my surprise, she continued to maintain her relationship with her father. Her father had expressed his love for her, but he sometimes did hurtful things. One day, she had dropped off a cooler of frozen fish. The cooler represented a summer's effort of fishing. Furthermore, she entrusted her summer's work to her father, who had indicated that he would prepare and smoke the fruit of her labors.

When she went back to his house and inquired about the fish, he merely responded that they were gone! Apparently, he had allowed the fish to spoil. I inquired how she felt about the situation, knowing I would have been upset.

Coolly and calmly, she said she had chosen not to react in a negative way. They were only fish, and her relationship with her father was more important. Not responding in a negative way freed her to establish a healthy response. We went on to discuss how unhealthy people don't know how to love in healthy ways. I believe her father was such a person.

To maintain her relationship with him, she guards her boundaries and does not allow herself to fall into the old family trap that ignites unhealthy responses. She has learned that her choices dictate whether she is to be blessed or cursed. Her wisdom has grown beyond her years and the many hurtful things she had to endure early in life. She has learned to avoid the weeds and stay focused on the wheat. This is a lesson that appears to be elusive in the lives of many people.

Choice is at the very heart of being human and being made in the image of God. We are able to make choices in our lives because this is God's gift to us. We choose, we act, and we decide because God has given us freedom to live our lives as we want.

When we embrace this freedom, we grow to accept three important aspects of making a decision. First, whenever faced with a decision, we always have a number of actions or persons from which to choose. Secondly, we are not tied to circumstances that take away our freedom to act. In every circumstance, there is a decision to be made. Thirdly, the choice of action will always have the desired effect—and that effect is encapsulated in the decision. In other words, we receive that which we choose. We must keep in mind that with every decision, there is responsibility—and consequences of our actions.

If we choose to love, we will find love. In finding love, we must also be the source of love. If we seek to be joyful, then we will uncover the joyful moments that life has to offer. In experiencing joy, it behooves us to instill joy in those who gather around us. If it is peace that we long for, then peace will find its way into our hearts. In experiencing peace, we must take on the responsibility of being peacemakers. If it is patience that eludes us, our decisions will help us to learn patience. Patience is a gift we can model for the world around us.

If we have battled the world around us, been fighting ourselves, or have waged war against God, then we can choose to view our battles from a different perspective. In viewing the world differently, we are called upon to change our perspective and cease our destructive ways. If our souls yearn for goodness, then we choose to embrace the Christ whose goodness is there for the asking. To embrace goodness, we take on the responsibility to be ambassadors of justice, mercy, compassion, and righteousness.

If our lives are out of control, then the fruits of God's spirit can bring us back in control. Self-control carries the responsibility to choose to live and embrace the Spirit of God—not according to our wants and desires. Each of the aforementioned gifts is within the reach of every human being, and they are but one decision removed from achieving them. We make the choice, but the outcome has been preordained by God since the beginning of time.

When we explore the biblical meaning of the word choice, this word is intimately connected to the word "elect." A central point in both the Old and New Testaments is that we are chosen by God. We are his elect. Election by God—for a people or nation—is made up of three elements. First, when God elects you, his choice is irrevocable. God cannot go back on his word, because his word is innate to his character.

Secondly, when you are a component of his election, his choice is based on his grace—not on who we are or what we have done or accomplished. Election is born out of God's freedom of choice, and his choice is grounded in his love for his creation and his beloved people. In choosing us, God has always encouraged his people to make the right choices for they are a matter of life and death.

In the Scriptures, story after story illustrates how God lays before his people the importance of their decisions. As Israel is preparing to cross over from the wilderness into the Promised Land, Moses reminds them of their covenant before God. God's covenant outlined blessings and curses. In the closing of chapter thirty, we find a powerful reminder.

> See, I set before you today life and prosperity, death, and destruction. For I command you today to love the Lord your God, to walk in his ways, and to keep his commands, decrees, and laws; then you will live and increase, the Lord your God will bless you in the land you are entering to possess.
>
> But if your heart turns away and you are not obedient, and if you are drawn away

to bow down to other gods and worship them, I declare to you this day that you will certainly be destroyed. You will not live long in the land you are crossing the Jordan to enter and possess.

This day I call heaven and earth as witnesses against you that I have set before you life and death, blessings, and curses. Now choose life, so that you and your children may live and that you may love the Lord your God, listen to his voice, and hold fast to him. For the Lord is your life, and he will give you many years in the land he swore to give to your fathers, Abraham, Isaac, and Jacob. (Deut. 30:11f)

In reading this account, we recognize that this statement is based on the covenant agreement between God and Israel. In addition, the blessings and curses are a condition upon Israel's obedience to God's law. If they obey the law, they will be blessed; if they stray from his word, they will face the consequences.

Although this agreement is a stipulation upon entering the land, we can hear a prophetic voice rise from the pages. As mentioned in a previous chapter, the land flowing with milk and honey, a new Garden of Eden, is a metaphor for the kingdom of heaven. As Israel was called into obedience as she entered the land, we are called into obedience if we are to experience the kingdom of God in our lives. .

In making the right choices, we reap the benefits of blessing. And in choosing the wrong path, we condemn ourselves—we separate ourselves from God and subject ourselves to a curse! The circumstances of this story have changed, but the results remain the same.

Making right choices was a critical component in early Hebrew culture. Their society and faith would not survive if they failed to teach their children. If they lost just one generation, all future generations would be lost—and it would take incredible energy to recover. Therefore, a father had a sacred duty to teach his children. Much of this teaching was formulated in the Book of Wisdom.

The Book of Wisdom, although attributed to King Solomon, was written by a circle of wise men. This incredible book of instruction contains a number of short teachings that develop in the faith community and those that were borrowed from Egypt. Whatever their source, the book illumines truth about the human experience; its words are designed to guide people to a blessed life.

Just listen and try to imagine sitting at the feet of your father with the rest of your siblings gathered around. The sun is getting ready to set and, as is his custom, he offers a nightly teaching in preparation for evening prayers. You are struck by his words as he personifies wisdom. His teaching reaches into your inner soul, grasping the profundity of his thoughts. The words are burned into your memory.

> Does not wisdom call out? Does not understanding raise her voice? On the heights along the way, where the paths meet, she takes her stand; beside the gates leading into the city, at the entrance, she cries aloud: I raise my voice to all mankind. To you, O men I call out; I raise my voice to all mankind.
>
> You who are simple, gain prudence; you who are foolish, gain understanding.
>
> Listen, for I have worthy things to say; I open my lips to speak what is right.
>
> My mouth speaks what is true, for my lips detest wickedness.

All the words of my mouth are just; none of them is crooked or perverse.

To the discerning all of them are right; they are faultless to those who have knowledge

Choose my instruction instead of silver, knowledge rather than choice gold, for wisdom is more precious than rubies, and nothing you desire can compare to her.

I, wisdom, dwell together with prudence; I possess knowledge and discretion.

To fear the Lord is to hate evil; I hate pride and arrogance, evil behavior and perverse speech.

Council and sound judgment are mine: I have understanding and power.

By me kings reign and rulers make laws that are just; by me princes govern and all nobles who rule on earth.

I love those who love me, and those who seek me find me.

With me are riches and honor, enduring wealth and prosperity.

My fruit is better than fine gold; what I yield surpasses choice silver.

I walk the way of the righteousness, along the paths of justice, bestowing wealth on those who love me and making their treasures full.

The Lord brought me forth as the first of his works, before deeds of old; I was appointed from eternity, from the beginning before the world began.

When there were no oceans, I was given birth, when there were no springs abounding with water: before the mountains were settled in places, before the hills, I was given birth, before he made the earth or its fields or any of the dust of the world.

I was there when he set the heavens in place, when he marked out the horizons on the face of the deep, when he established the clouds above and fixed securely the fountains of deep, when he gave the sea its boundary so the water would not overstep his command, and when the he marked out foundations of the earth.

Then I was the craftsman at his side.

I was filled with delight day after day, rejoicing always in his presence, rejoicing in his whole world and delighting in mankind.

Now then, my sons, listen to me; blessed are those who keep my ways.

Listen to my instruction and be wise do not ignore it.

Blessed is the man who listens to me, watching daily at my doors, waiting at my doorway.

For whoever finds me finds life and receives favor from the Lord.

But whoever fails to find me harms himself: all who hate me love death. (Prov. 8)

In pondering these words and thinking back to my youth, I cannot ever remember my father teaching us the words of wisdom and their effect on our lives. Even though he read the Bible daily, I suspect that faith was an individual journey that remained a private excursion. This is not to say he never taught us the difference between right and wrong and moral responsibility. He taught us many things—how to fish, tend a flower garden, repair things, drive a car, and proper social behavior. He made sure that we were instructed about religion, but he never opened the discussion himself.

Wisdom, and its intimate connection to blessings, was a topic that eluded our family conversations. I had to search for myself, which meant I stumbled many times along the way. On many occasions, I found myself in the weeds—not knowing how I got there or how to choose a path to draw me out.

There comes a time in the lives of men and women when we must concede that we make poor choices and live our lives in a faulty reality that is seeded with landmines. At best, many people escape the physical and emotional damage for a while, but the time comes when their world implodes. Unfortunately, they need to reach the tipping point and crash before they are ready for a midcourse correction in their lives. Only then will they will open their souls in search of a new paradigm that will be filled with blessing.

Finding this new paradigm is not an easy process; it requires going against every inclination we have come to accept. Finding a new paradigm requires changing our patterns of thinking, which affects how we feel and act. Jesus said, "You must be born again" (John 3:3). The teacher, Nicodemus, thought that Jesus was speaking physically; however, Jesus was speaking metaphorically and referring to a spiritual rebirth.

The first lesson we have to learn is that we live in a world filled with paradox. When it comes to the kingdom of God, the blessings are forthcoming. Given the fact that God is ultimately a mystery, we will never fully grasp his thoughts and nature. Yes, Christians believe that God has revealed enough of himself in Christ to provide salvation, but we will never know his full nature until we have passed from this world into the next. If we can live with the reality of mystery and paradox, we can begin to explore our new journey. Though filled with surprises, we are in store for an exciting ride as God moves us in directions we would not choose for ourselves.

What may we conclude? In moving in new directions, we will be forced to take a second look at what is described as a blessing—and we will redefine what we consider a curse. In probing the world of blessings and curses, we will learn patience because, like the wheat and the weeds, we cannot distinguish one from the other in their early forms of development. Yet, we are not left in the dark.

Through the Scriptures, we can identify the core values of blessing and embrace them in our lives. These Scriptures have revealed that God has a will and purpose in our lives. Equally as important, his voice can be heard through his encounters with his creation and with those who dare to stop and listen. In listening to his voice, we recognize the choices before us. We can fully grasp that the choices we make in life have consequences; these decisions can open the doors of a blessed or a cursed life.

As easy as this journey sounds on paper, it is laden with twist and turns. It is no wonder that we can find ourselves off course and in the weeds. One would be wise to utilize a guide, mentor, coach, or spiritual director when entering unchartered territory. Those who invite guides into their lives must remember that a guide must be spiritually mature and have the ability to transform knowledge into wisdom.

These guides don't tell us where we need to go; they are invited into our lives to help us find God's path for ourselves. As they illumine a path, their words will ring true in our hearts. Their insights uncover for us the latent fingerprints of the world of wisdom, revealing the unmistakable sounds of truth. This truth is God's truth; he uses these guides as instruments of his grace. As instruments of divine grace, the truth that is revealed will never contradict what God has already revealed. God cannot—and will not—reverse his Word. He always needs to be true to himself if we are to trust in him. We can trust in all his promises.

We can trust that his deepest desire is that we live a blessed life. To experience the blessed life, he promises that if we live by his Word, then the world of blessing is uncovered. The world of blessing is available to all who seek and wish to accept the invitation from God to enter into his presence.

Our journey to the divine is a walk in faith because life will continue to offer challenges. But with God nothing is wasted—and nothing is lost! When we choose to walk into his presence, God will provide teachable moments that allow us to discover the rich reality of his kingdom.

In these teachable moments, we will encounter suffering from time to time. We will discover that our journey is made perfect by our suffering (Heb. 2:10). God has promised us his divine protection, which gives us the courage to move forward. We move forward because there is no future in looking back—except to look back to the cross of Christ, which marks the guarantee of victory that has already been accomplished on our behalf.

The kingdom of God has come. It is a present reality that is filled with his blessing! All we have to do is choose life! And learn to walk through the weeds.

BIBLIOGRAPHY

Dodd, C. H. *The Interpretation of the Fourth Gospel*, Cambridge: Cambridge University Press, 1968.

Guiley, Rosemary Ellen. *The Quotable Saints*. NY: Checkmark Books, 2002.

The New International Dictionary of New Testament Theology: Vol. 1, Vol. 2. General Editor, Colin Brown. Grand Rapids, Michigan: Zondervan, 1976.

The NIV Study Bible: New International Version. Edited by Kenneth Baker. Grand Rapids, Michigan: Zondervan Publishing, 1985.

Prager, Rabbi Marica. *The Path of Blessing*. Woodstock, VT: Jewish Light Publishing, 1998.

Smalley, Gary and John Trent, PhD. *The Gift of the Blessing.* Nashville, TN: Thomas Nelson, 1993.

Thompson Chain-Reference Bible. New International Version. Edited by Frank Charles Thompson. Grand Rapids Michigan. Zondervan Publishing, 1983.

ABOUT THE AUTHOR

LAWRENCE Perry shares his unique insights after experiencing twenty-six years of parish ministry. After graduation from Trinity School for Ministry in Ambridge, Pennsylvania, with a Masters of Divinity Degree, he served a number of churches—small and large, rural and urban.

In addition, his insights were further enriched by his ten years of experience as a deputy sheriff, police officer, and investigator in California and Wyoming. Adding to his experience is his work with those in the recovery community. Perry provided spiritual direction for those suffering from alcohol and drug addiction. He also has conducted a number of lectures and workshops on codependency. Through his vast experience, he encountered many men and women who found themselves in the midst of the weeds.

In his book, he extracts his own experience—and those of his family and friends—to articulate the courses of blessings and curses. Using the Scriptures, he weaves together the wisdom of God's Word with personal stories to give his audience a profound understanding of the parable of the wheat and the weeds in Matthew's gospel.

Lawrence Perry lives in Colorado with his wife, Margretta, and their Springer Spaniel, Emily. Though retired from ministry, he continues his outreach to others through his writing, volunteering, and life coaching practice.

Perry served in the United States Air Force and in Vietnam,1966. He is the father of two children, Alejandrina and Tony. In addition, he and Margretta helped raise three foster children.

www.ingramcontent.com/pod-product-compliance
Lightning Source LLC
Chambersburg PA
CBHW022249290526
45785CB00015B/433